GRANDMA'S CASSEROLES

Laurie Korsgaden Watercolors

pil

Publications International, Ltd.

Favorite Brand Name Recipes at www.fbnr.com

ISBN: 0-7853-8646-7

Library of Congress Control Number: 2002117494

Manufactured in China.

8 7 6 5 4 3 2 1

Microwave Cooking: Microwave ovens vary in wattage. Use the cooking times as guidelines and check for doneness before adding more time.

Preparation/Cooking Times: Preparation times are based on the approximate amount of time required to assemble the recipe before cooking, baking, chilling or serving. These times include preparation steps such as measuring, chopping and mixing. The fact that some preparations and cooking can be done simultaneously is taken into account. Preparation of optional ingredients and serving suggestions is not included.

GRANDMA'S CASSEROLES

Ham and Cheese Bread Pudding

1 small loaf (8 ounces) sourdough, country French
 or Italian bread, cut into 1-inch-thick slices

3 tablespoons butter or margarine, softened

8 ounces ham or smoked ham, cubed

2 cups (8 ounces) shredded mild or sharp Cheddar
 cheese

3 eggs

2 cups milk

1 teaspoon dry mustard

½ teaspoon salt

⅛ teaspoon white pepper

1. Grease 11×7-inch baking dish. Spread 1 side of each bread slice with butter. Cut into 1-inch cubes; place on bottom of prepared dish. Top with ham; sprinkle with cheese.

2. Beat eggs in medium bowl. Whisk in milk, mustard, salt and pepper. Pour egg mixture evenly over bread mixture. Cover; refrigerate at least 6 hours or overnight.

3. Preheat oven to 350°F.

4. Bake bread pudding, uncovered, 45 to 50 minutes or until puffed and golden brown and knife inserted into center comes out clean. Garnish, if desired. Cut into squares. Serve immediately.   *Makes 8 servings*

Ham and Cheese Bread Pudding

Brunch Strata Breakfast

2 bags SUCCESS® Rice

   Vegetable cooking spray

2 eggs

8 slices (⅔ ounce *each*) reduced-fat Swiss cheese

½ pound turkey ham, chopped

1 can (7 ounces) whole kernel corn, drained

½ cup chopped onion

2 cups skim milk

1 cup (8 ounces) liquid egg substitute

1 teaspoon salt

¼ teaspoon pepper

Prepare rice according to package directions.

Preheat oven to 350°F. Spray 13×9-inch baking dish with cooking spray; set aside.

Slightly beat eggs with fork. Add rice; mix well. Press rice mixture onto bottom of prepared baking dish. Cover with cheese slices; top with ham, corn and onion. Combine milk and egg substitute; pour over ham. Sprinkle with salt and pepper. Bake until center is set, about 35 minutes. Let stand 5 minutes before cutting to serve.

Makes 8 servings

Hash Brown Casserole

3 cartons (4 ounces *each*) cholesterol-free egg
   product or 6 large eggs, well beaten
1 can (12 fluid ounces) NESTLÉ® CARNATION®
   Evaporated Milk
1 teaspoon salt
½ teaspoon ground black pepper
1 package (30 ounces) frozen shredded hash brown
   potatoes
2 cups (8 ounces) shredded cheddar cheese
1 medium onion, chopped
1 small green bell pepper, chopped
1 cup diced ham (optional)

PREHEAT oven to 350°F. Grease 13×9-inch baking
dish.

COMBINE egg product, evaporated milk, salt and black
pepper in large bowl. Add potatoes, cheese, onion, bell
pepper and ham; mix well. Pour mixture into prepared
baking dish.

BAKE for 60 to 65 minutes or until set.

Makes 12 servings

Note: For a lower fat version of this recipe, use the
cholesterol-free egg product, substitute NESTLÉ
CARNATION® Evaporated Fat Free Milk for Evaporated
Milk and 10 slices turkey bacon, cooked and chopped, for
the diced ham. Proceed as above.

Bacon and Maple Grits Puff

8 slices bacon
2 cups milk
1¼ cups water
1 cup quick-cooking grits
½ teaspoon salt
½ cup pure maple syrup
4 eggs
Fresh chives (optional)

1. Preheat oven to 350°F. Grease 1½-quart round casserole or soufflé dish; set aside. Cook bacon in large skillet over medium-high heat about 7 minutes or until crisp. Remove bacon to paper towel; set aside. Reserve 2 tablespoons bacon drippings.

2. Combine milk, water, grits and salt in medium saucepan. Bring to a boil over medium heat, stirring frequently. Simmer 2 to 3 minutes or until mixture thickens, stirring constantly. Remove from heat; stir in syrup and reserved 2 tablespoons bacon drippings.

3. Crumble bacon; reserve ¼ cup for garnish. Stir remaining crumbled bacon into grits mixture.

4. Beat eggs in medium bowl. Gradually stir small amount of grits mixture into eggs, then stir back into remaining grits mixture. Pour into prepared casserole.

5. Bake 1 hour and 20 minutes or until knife inserted into center comes out clean. Top with reserved ¼ cup bacon. Garnish with fresh chives, if desired. Serve immediately.

Makes 6 to 8 servings

Note: Puff will fall slightly after removing from oven.

Bacon and Maple Grits Puff

Make-Ahead Brunch Bake

1 pound bulk pork sausage

6 eggs, beaten

2 cups light cream or half-and-half

1 teaspoon ground mustard

½ teaspoon salt

1 cup (4 ounces) shredded Cheddar cheese, divided

1⅓ cups *French's®* French Fried Onions, divided

Crumble sausage into large skillet. Cook over medium-high heat until browned; drain well. Stir in eggs, cream, mustard, salt, ½ cup cheese and ⅔ *cup* French Fried Onions; mix well. Pour into greased 8×12-inch baking dish. Refrigerate, covered, 8 hours or overnight. Bake, uncovered, at 350°F for 45 minutes or until knife inserted into center comes out clean. Top with remaining ½ cup cheese and ⅔ *cup* onions; bake, uncovered, 5 minutes or until onions are golden brown. Let stand 15 minutes before serving. *Makes 6 servings*

Microwave Directions: Crumble sausage into 12×8-inch microwave-safe dish. Microwave, covered, on HIGH 4 to 6 minutes or until sausage is cooked. Stir sausage halfway through cooking time. Drain well. Stir in ingredients and refrigerate as above. Microwave, covered, 10 to 15 minutes or until center is firm. Stir egg mixture halfway through cooking time. Top with remaining cheese and onions; cook, uncovered, 1 minute or until cheese melts. Let stand 5 minutes.

Cheesy Ham Casserole

2 cups fresh or frozen broccoli flowerets, thawed

1½ cups KRAFT® Shredded Sharp Cheddar Cheese, divided

1½ cups coarsely chopped ham

1½ cups (4 ounces) corkscrew pasta, cooked, drained

½ cup MIRACLE WHIP® or MIRACLE WHIP® LIGHT® Dressing

½ green or red bell pepper, chopped

¼ cup milk

Seasoned croutons (optional)

- Heat oven to 350°F.

- Mix all ingredients except ½ cup cheese and croutons.

- Spoon into 1½-quart casserole. Sprinkle with remaining ½ cup cheese.

- Bake 30 minutes or until thoroughly heated. Sprinkle with croutons, if desired.   *Makes 4 to 6 servings*

Prep Time: 15 minutes
Cook Time: 30 minutes

11

Country Fare Breakfast with Wisconsin Fontina

¼ cup butter

2 cups frozen hash brown potatoes

¼ cup finely chopped onion

6 eggs, beaten

2 tablespoons milk

¾ teaspoon salt

⅛ teaspoon pepper

¼ cup chopped parsley, divided

1 cup (4 ounces) shredded Wisconsin Fontina cheese, divided

1 cup cubed cooked turkey

Melt butter in 10-inch ovenproof skillet; add potatoes and onion. Cook, covered, over medium heat 15 minutes until tender and lightly browned; stir occasionally. Beat together eggs, milk, salt and pepper; stir in 3 tablespoons parsley and ½ cup cheese. Pour egg mixture over potatoes; sprinkle with turkey. Bake, uncovered, in preheated 350°F oven for 20 minutes or until eggs are set. Sprinkle remaining ½ cup cheese over eggs; return to oven for about 2 minutes until cheese is melted. Remove from oven and garnish with remaining 1 tablespoon parsley. Cut into wedges and serve with salsa, if desired.

Makes 6 servings

Note: Ham may be substituted for turkey.

Favorite recipe from **Wisconsin Milk Marketing Board**

Country Fare Breakfast with Wisconsin Fontina

French Toast Strata

4 cups (4 ounces) day-old French or Italian bread, cut into ¾-inch cubes

⅓ cup golden raisins

1 package (3 ounces) cream cheese, cut into ¼-inch cubes

3 eggs

1½ cups milk

½ cup maple-flavored pancake syrup

1 teaspoon vanilla

2 tablespoons sugar

1 teaspoon ground cinnamon

Additional maple-flavored pancake syrup (optional)

1. Spray 11×7-inch baking dish with nonstick cooking spray. Place bread cubes in even layer in prepared dish; sprinkle raisins and cream cheese evenly over bread.

2. Beat eggs in medium bowl with electric mixer at medium speed until blended. Add milk, ½ cup pancake syrup and vanilla; mix well. Pour egg mixture evenly over bread mixture. Cover; refrigerate at least 4 hours or overnight.

3. Preheat oven to 350°F. Combine sugar and cinnamon in small bowl; sprinkle evenly over strata.

4. Bake, uncovered, 40 to 45 minutes or until puffed, golden brown and knife inserted into center comes out clean. Cut into squares and serve with additional pancake syrup, if desired. *Makes 6 servings*

French Toast Strata

Ham & Cheese Grits Soufflé

   3 cups water
   ¾ cup quick-cooking grits
   ½ teaspoon salt
   ½ cup (2 ounces) shredded mozzarella cheese
   2 ounces ham, finely chopped
   2 tablespoons minced chives
   2 eggs, separated
   Dash hot pepper sauce

1. Preheat oven to 375°F. Grease 1½-quart soufflé dish or deep casserole.

2. Bring water to a boil in medium saucepan. Stir in grits and salt. Cook, stirring frequently, about 5 minutes or until thickened. Stir in cheese, ham, chives, egg yolks and hot pepper sauce.

3. In small clean bowl, beat egg whites until stiff but not dry; fold into grits mixture. Pour into prepared dish. Bake about 30 minutes or until puffed and golden. Serve immediately.   *Makes 4 to 6 servings*

Double Cheese Strata

10 to 12 slices Italian bread, about ½ inch thick

⅔ cup (about 5 ounces) sharp Cheddar light cold pack cheese food, softened

1⅓ cups *French's®* French Fried Onions

1 package (10 ounces) frozen chopped broccoli, thawed and drained

½ cup (2 ounces) shredded Swiss cheese

5 eggs

3 cups milk

2 tablespoons *French's®* Zesty Deli Mustard

½ teaspoon salt

¼ teaspoon ground white pepper

Grease 3-quart baking dish. Spread bread slices with Cheddar cheese. Arrange slices in a single layer in bottom of prepared baking dish, pressing to fit. Layer French Fried Onions, broccoli and Swiss cheese over bread.

Beat together eggs, milk, mustard, salt and pepper in medium bowl until well blended. Pour egg mixture over layers. Let stand 10 minutes. Preheat oven to 350°F. Bake 35 minutes or until knife inserted into center comes out clean. (Cover loosely with foil near end of baking if top becomes too brown.) Cool on wire rack 10 minutes. Cut into squares to serve. *Makes 8 servings*

Prep Time: 15 minutes
Cook Time: 35 minutes
Stand Time: 10 minutes

17

Beef & Zucchini Quiche

1 unbaked 9-inch pie shell

½ pound lean ground beef

1 medium zucchini, shredded

3 green onions, sliced

¼ cup sliced mushrooms

1 tablespoon all-purpose flour

1 cup milk

3 eggs, beaten

¾ cup (3 ounces) shredded Swiss cheese

1½ teaspoons chopped fresh thyme *or* ½ teaspoon dried thyme leaves

½ teaspoon salt

Dash black pepper

Dash ground red pepper

1. Preheat oven to 475°F.

2. Line pie shell with foil; fill with dried beans or rice. Bake 8 minutes. Remove from oven; carefully remove foil and beans. Return pie shell to oven. Continue baking 4 minutes; set aside. *Reduce oven temperature to 375°F.*

3. Brown ground beef in medium skillet, stirring to break up meat; drain. Add zucchini, onions and mushrooms; cook, stirring occasionally, until vegetables are tender. Stir in flour; cook 2 minutes, stirring constantly. Remove from heat.

4. Combine milk, eggs, cheese and seasonings in medium bowl. Stir into ground beef mixture; pour into crust. Bake 35 minutes or until knife inserted near center comes out clean. *Makes 6 servings*

Mom's Favorite Brunch Casserole

6 eggs
1 cup plain yogurt
1 cup (4 ounces) shredded Cheddar cheese
½ teaspoon black pepper
1 cup finely chopped ham
½ can (8 ounces) pasteurized process cheese

1. Preheat oven to 350°F. Lightly grease 12×8-inch baking dish.

2. Combine eggs and yogurt in medium bowl; beat with wire whisk until well blended. Stir in Cheddar cheese and pepper.

3. Place ham in prepared baking dish; pour egg mixture over ham. Bake 25 to 30 minutes or until egg mixture is set. Use process cheese to write "MOM" or other desired message to Mom on top of casserole; let stand 2 to 3 minutes or until cheese is slightly melted.

Makes 10 servings

Variation: Substitute 1 pound bulk pork sausage, browned and drained, for ham.

Make-Ahead Breakfast Casserole

2½ cups seasoned croutons
1 pound BOB EVANS® Original Recipe Roll Sausage
2¼ cups milk
4 eggs
1 (10½-ounce) can condensed cream of mushroom soup
1 (10-ounce) package frozen chopped spinach, thawed and squeezed dry
1 (4-ounce) can mushrooms, drained and chopped
1 cup (4 ounces) shredded sharp Cheddar cheese
1 cup (4 ounces) shredded Monterey Jack cheese
¼ teaspoon dry mustard
Fresh herb sprigs and carrot strips (optional)
Picante sauce or salsa (optional)

Spread croutons on bottom of greased 13×9-inch baking dish. Crumble sausage into medium skillet. Cook over medium heat until browned, stirring occasionally. Drain off any drippings. Spread over croutons. Whisk milk and eggs in large bowl until blended. Stir in soup, spinach, mushrooms, cheeses and mustard. Pour egg mixture over sausage and croutons. Refrigerate overnight. Preheat oven to 325°F. Bake egg mixture 50 to 55 minutes or until set and lightly browned on top. Garnish with herb sprigs and carrot, if desired. Serve hot with picante sauce, if desired. Refrigerate leftovers. *Makes 10 to 12 servings*

Make-Ahead Breakfast Casserole

Potato Breakfast Custard

3 large Colorado russet variety potatoes, peeled and
   thinly sliced

   Salt and black pepper

8 ounces low-fat bulk sausage, cooked and
   crumbled*

⅓ cup roasted red bell pepper, thinly sliced, *or* 1 jar
   (2 ounces) sliced pimientos, drained

3 eggs

1 cup low-fat (1%) milk

3 tablespoons chopped chives or green onion tops

¾ teaspoon dried thyme or oregano leaves, crushed

   Salsa and sour cream (optional)

*Substitute 6 ounces finely diced lean ham or 6 ounces crumbled, cooked turkey
bacon for sausage, if desired.*

Preheat oven to 375°F. Butter 8- or 9-inch square baking
dish or other small casserole. Arrange ½ of potatoes in
baking dish. Season to taste with salt and black pepper.
Cover with ½ of sausage. Arrange remaining potatoes over
sausage; season to taste with salt and black pepper. Top
with remaining sausage and red peppers. Beat eggs, milk,
chives and thyme until blended. Pour over potatoes.
Cover baking dish with foil and bake 45 to 50 minutes
or until potatoes are tender. Uncover and bake 5 to
10 minutes longer. Serve with salsa and sour cream, if
desired.   *Makes 4 to 5 servings*

Favorite recipe from **Colorado Potato Administrative Committee**

Potato Breakfast Custard

Cheesy Country SPAM™ Puff

6 slices white bread, torn into small pieces
1¼ cups milk
3 eggs
1 tablespoon spicy mustard
½ teaspoon garlic powder
½ teaspoon paprika
1 (12-ounce) can SPAM® Classic, cubed
2 cups (8 ounces) shredded sharp Cheddar cheese, divided
½ cup chopped onion
½ cup (2 ounces) shredded Monterey Jack cheese

Heat oven to 375°F. In large bowl, combine bread, milk, eggs, mustard, garlic powder and paprika. Beat at medium speed of electric mixer 1 minute or until smooth. Stir in SPAM®, 1 cup Cheddar cheese and onion. Pour into greased 12×8-inch baking dish. Bake 25 minutes. Top with remaining 1 cup Cheddar cheese and Monterey Jack cheese. Bake 5 minutes longer or until cheese is melted. Let stand 10 minutes before serving.   *Makes 8 servings*

Cheesy Country SPAM™ Puff

Spinach Sensation

½ pound bacon slices

1 cup (8 ounces) sour cream

3 eggs, separated

2 tablespoons all-purpose flour

⅛ teaspoon black pepper

1 package (10 ounces) frozen chopped spinach,
   thawed and squeezed dry

½ cup (2 ounces) shredded sharp Cheddar cheese

½ cup dry bread crumbs

1 tablespoon margarine or butter, melted

1. Preheat oven to 350°F. Spray 2-quart round baking dish with nonstick cooking spray.

2. Place bacon in single layer in large skillet; cook over medium heat until crisp. Remove from skillet; drain on paper towels. Crumble and set aside.

3. Combine sour cream, egg yolks, flour and pepper in large bowl; set aside. Beat egg whites in medium bowl with electric mixer at high speed until stiff peaks form. Stir ¼ of egg whites into sour cream mixture; fold in remaining egg whites.

4. Arrange half of spinach in prepared dish. Top with half of sour cream mixture. Sprinkle ¼ cup cheese over sour cream mixture. Sprinkle bacon over cheese. Repeat layers, ending with remaining ¼ cup cheese.

5. Combine bread crumbs and margarine in small bowl; sprinkle evenly over cheese. Bake, uncovered, 30 to 35 minutes or until egg mixture is set. Let stand 5 minutes before serving.   *Makes 6 servings*

Spinach Sensation

Easy-to-Fix Casseroles

Cheesy Broccoli Bake

1 (10-ounce) package frozen chopped broccoli
1 (10¾-ounce) can condensed Cheddar cheese soup
½ cup sour cream
2 cups (12 ounces) chopped CURE 81® ham
2 cups cooked rice
½ cup soft, torn bread crumbs
1 tablespoon butter or margarine, melted

Heat oven to 350°F. Cook broccoli according to package directions; drain. Combine soup and sour cream. Stir in broccoli, ham and rice. Spoon into 1½-quart casserole. Combine bread crumbs and butter; sprinkle over casserole. Bake 30 to 35 minutes or until thoroughly heated.

Makes 4 to 6 servings

28

Cheesy Broccoli Bake

1-2-3 Cheddar Broccoli Casserole

1 jar (16 ounces) RAGÚ® Cheese Creations!®
  Double Cheddar Sauce
2 boxes (10 ounces each) frozen broccoli florets,
  thawed
¼ cup plain or Italian seasoned dry bread crumbs
1 tablespoon margarine or butter, melted

Preheat oven to 350°F. In 1½-quart casserole, combine Ragú Cheese Creations! Sauce and broccoli.

Evenly top with bread crumbs combined with margarine.

Bake, uncovered, 20 minutes or until bread crumbs are golden and broccoli is tender.   *Makes 6 servings*

Tip: Substitute your favorite frozen vegetables or vegetable blend for broccoli florets.

Prep Time: 5 minutes
Cook Time: 20 minutes

1-2-3 Cheddar Broccoli Casserole

Herbed Chicken and Potatoes

2 medium all-purpose potatoes, thinly sliced (about 1 pound)

4 bone-in chicken breast halves (about 2 pounds)*

1 envelope LIPTON® RECIPE SECRETS® Savory Herb with Garlic Soup Mix

⅓ cup water

1 tablespoon olive or vegetable oil

*Substitution: Use 1 (2½- to 3-pound) chicken, cut into serving pieces.

1. Preheat oven to 425°F. In 13×9-inch baking or roasting pan, add potatoes; arrange chicken over potatoes.

2. Pour soup mix blended with water and oil over chicken and potatoes.

3. Bake, uncovered, 40 minutes or until chicken is no longer pink and potatoes are tender.   *Makes 4 servings*

Family Baked Bean Dinner

1 can (20 ounces) DOLE® Pineapple Chunks
½ DOLE® Green Bell Pepper, julienne-cut
½ cup chopped onion
1 pound Polish sausage or frankfurters, cut into
    1-inch chunks
⅓ cup packed brown sugar
1 teaspoon dry mustard
2 cans (16 ounces each) baked beans

Microwave Directions
• Drain pineapple chunks; reserve juice for beverage. Set aside. Add green pepper and onion to 13×9-inch microwavable dish.

• Cover; microwave on HIGH (100% power) 3 minutes. Add sausage, arranging around edges of dish. Cover; continue microwaving on HIGH (100% power) 6 minutes.

• In bowl, combine brown sugar and mustard; stir in beans and reserved pineapple. Add to sausage mixture. Stir to combine. Microwave, uncovered, on HIGH (100% power) 8 to 10 minutes, stirring after 4 minutes.

Makes 6 servings

Velveeta® Spicy Chicken Spaghetti

12 ounces spaghetti, uncooked

4 boneless skinless chicken breast halves (about 1¼ pounds), cut into strips

1 pound (16 ounces) VELVEETA® Pasteurized Prepared Cheese Product, cut up

1 can (10¾ ounces) condensed cream of chicken soup

1 can (10 ounces) diced tomatoes and green chilies, undrained

1 can (4½ ounces) sliced mushrooms, drained

⅓ cup milk

1. Cook pasta as directed on package; drain. Return to same pan.

2. Spray skillet with no stick cooking spray. Add chicken; cook and stir on medium-high heat 4 to 5 minutes or until cooked through. Add VELVEETA, soup, tomatoes and green chilies, mushrooms and milk; stir on low heat until VELVEETA is melted. Add chicken mixture to pasta; toss to coat. Spoon into greased 13×9-inch baking dish.

3. Bake at 350°F for 35 to 40 minutes or until hot.

Makes 6 to 8 servings

Prep Time: 25 minutes
Bake Time: 40 minutes

Velveeta® Spicy Chicken Spaghetti

Cheesy Chicken Pot Pie

1 pound boneless, skinless chicken breast halves, cut
  into ½-inch chunks
1 tablespoon all-purpose flour
1 jar (16 ounces) RAGÚ® Cheese Creations!®
  Double Cheddar Sauce
1 bag (16 ounces) frozen mixed vegetables, thawed
1 prepared pastry for single-crust pie

Preheat oven to 425°F. In 2-quart casserole, toss chicken
with flour. Stir in Ragú Cheese Creations! Sauce and
vegetables. Cover casserole with prepared pastry. Press
pastry around edge of casserole to seal; trim excess pastry,
then flute edges. Cover with aluminum foil and bake
20 minutes. Remove foil and continue baking 20 minutes
or until crust is golden and chicken is no longer pink. Let
stand 5 minutes before serving.   *Makes 6 servings*

Grandma's Tip

*This is the perfect dish for leftovers. Substitute
cooked pork roast, turkey breast or even roast
beef for the chicken.*

36

Cheesy Chicken Pot Pie

Original Green Bean Casserole

- 1 can (10¾ ounces) condensed cream of mushroom soup
- ¾ cup milk
- ⅛ teaspoon pepper
- 2 packages (9 ounces each) frozen cut green beans, thawed*
- 1⅓ cups *French's*® French Fried Onions, divided

Substitute 2 cans (14½ ounces each) cut green beans, drained for frozen green beans.

1. Preheat oven to 350°F. Combine soup, milk and pepper in 1½-quart casserole; stir until well blended. Stir in beans and ⅔ *cup* French Fried Onions.

2. Bake, uncovered, 30 minutes or until hot; stir. Sprinkle with remaining ⅔ *cup* onions. Bake 5 minutes or until onions are golden brown.   *Makes 6 servings*

Microwave Directions: Prepare green bean mixture as above; pour into 1½-quart microwave-safe casserole. Cover with vented plastic wrap. Microwave on HIGH 8 to 10 minutes or until heated through, stirring halfway. Uncover. Top with remaining French Fried Onions. Cook 1 minute until onions are golden. Let stand 5 minutes.

Substitution: You may substitute 4 cups cooked, cut fresh green beans for the frozen or canned.

Prep Time: 5 minutes
Cook Time: 35 minutes

Creamed Spinach Casserole

2 packages (10 ounces each) frozen chopped
    spinach, thawed, well drained

2 packages (8 ounces each) PHILADELPHIA®
    Cream Cheese, softened

1 teaspoon lemon and pepper seasoning salt

⅓ cup crushed seasoned croutons

MIX spinach, cream cheese and seasoning salt until well blended.

SPOON into 1-quart casserole. Sprinkle with crushed croutons.

BAKE at 350°F for 25 to 30 minutes or until thoroughly heated.
Makes 6 to 8 servings

Prep Time: 10 minutes
Bake Time: 30 minutes

Saucy Garden Patch
Vegetables

1 can (10¾ ounces) condensed Cheddar cheese soup

½ cup sour cream

¼ cup milk

1 bag (16 ounces) frozen vegetable combination,
such as broccoli, corn and red bell pepper,
thawed and drained

1 bag (16 ounces) frozen vegetable combination,
such as brussels sprouts, carrots and cauliflower,
thawed and drained

1 cup (4 ounces) shredded Cheddar cheese

1⅓ cups *French's*® French Fried Onions, divided

Microwave Directions
Combine soup, sour cream and milk in large bowl. Stir in
vegetables, cheese and ⅔ *cup* French Fried Onions. Spoon
into microwavable 2-quart oblong baking dish.

Cover loosely with plastic wrap. Microwave on HIGH
10 minutes or until vegetables are tender and mixture is
heated through, stirring halfway through cooking time.
Uncover; sprinkle with remaining ⅔ *cup* onions.
Microwave on HIGH 1 minute or until onions are golden.

Makes 8 to 10 servings

Oven Directions: Prepare vegetable mixture as above.
Bake, covered, in 400°F oven 45 minutes or until tender
and mixture is heated through. Stir; sprinkle with
remaining onions. Bake, uncovered, 1 minute.

Saucy Garden Patch Vegetables

Pork Chops and Yams

4 pork chops (½ inch thick)

2 tablespoons oil

2 (16-ounce) cans yams or sweet potatoes, drained

¾ cup SMUCKER'S® Orange Marmalade or Apricot
   Preserves

½ large green bell pepper, cut into strips

2 tablespoons minced onion

1. Brown pork chops in oil over medium heat.

2. Place yams in 1½-quart casserole. Stir in marmalade, bell pepper and onion. Layer pork chops over yam mixture. Cover and bake at 350°F for 30 minutes or until pork chops are tender.   *Makes 4 servings*

Tuna Veg•All® Casserole

3 cups cooked egg noodles

1 can (15 ounces) VEG•ALL® Original Mixed
    Vegetables, with liquid

1 can (10¾ ounces) cream of mushroom soup

1 can (9 ounces) white tuna in water, drained

1 cup shredded cheddar cheese

Preheat oven to 350°F. Combine all ingredients in
1½-quart casserole. Bake for 30 minutes or until heated
through.   *Makes 6 servings*

Prep Time: 7 minutes

Turkey and Biscuits

2 cans (10¾ ounces each) condensed cream of
   chicken soup

¼ cup dry white wine

¼ teaspoon poultry seasoning

2 packages (8 ounces each) frozen cut asparagus,
   thawed

3 cups cubed cooked turkey or chicken

Paprika (optional)

1 can (11 ounces) refrigerated flaky biscuits

1. Preheat oven to 350°F. Spray 13×9-inch baking dish
with nonstick cooking spray.

2. Combine soup, wine and poultry seasoning in medium
bowl.

3. Arrange asparagus in single layer in prepared dish.
Place turkey evenly over asparagus. Spread soup mixture
over turkey. Sprinkle lightly with paprika, if desired.

4. Cover tightly with foil and bake 20 minutes. Remove
from oven. *Increase oven temperature to 425°F.* Top with
biscuits and bake, uncovered, 8 to 10 minutes or until
biscuits are golden brown.   *Makes 6 servings*

Turkey and Biscuit

Tomato Scalloped Potatoes

1 can (14½ ounces) DEL MONTE® Diced Tomatoes
1 pound red potatoes, thinly sliced
1 medium onion, chopped
½ cup whipping cream
1 cup (4 ounces) shredded Swiss cheese
3 tablespoons grated Parmesan cheese

1. Preheat oven to 350°F.

2. Drain tomatoes, reserving liquid; pour liquid into measuring cup. Add water to measure 1 cup.

3. Add reserved liquid, potatoes and onion to large skillet; cover. Cook 10 minutes or until tender.

4. Place potato mixture in 1-quart baking dish; top with tomatoes and cream. Sprinkle with cheeses.

5. Bake 20 minutes or until hot and bubbly. Sprinkle with chopped parsley, if desired. *Makes 6 servings*

Prep Time: 8 minutes
Cook Time: 30 minutes

Tomato Scalloped Potatoes

Creamy Beef and Vegetable Casserole

1 pound lean ground beef
1 small onion, chopped
1 bag (16 ounces) BIRDS EYE® frozen Farm Fresh
   Mixtures Broccoli, Corn & Red Peppers
1 can (10¾ ounces) cream of mushroom soup

• In medium skillet, brown beef and onion; drain excess fat.

• Meanwhile, in large saucepan, cook vegetables according to package directions; drain.

• Stir in beef mixture and soup. Cook over medium heat until heated through. *Makes 4 servings*

Serving Suggestion: Serve over rice and sprinkle with ½ cup shredded Cheddar cheese.

Prep Time: 5 minutes
Cook Time: 10 to 15 minutes

48

Ham Starburst Casserole

- 1 can (10¾ ounces) condensed cream of potato soup
- ¾ cup sour cream
- 1 can (16 ounces) sliced potatoes, drained
- 1 package (10 ounces) frozen peas, thawed and drained
- 1⅓ cups *French's*® French Fried Onions, divided
- 2 tablespoons diced pimiento (optional)
- 8 to 12 ounces cooked ham or turkey ham, unsliced

Preheat oven to 350°F. In medium bowl, combine soup, sour cream, potatoes, peas, ⅔ *cup* French Fried Onions and the pimiento; stir well. Spoon into 10-inch round baking dish. Cut ham into 3 thick slices; cut each slice crosswise into halves. Press ham slices into potato mixture, rounded-side up in spoke-fashion, to form a starburst. Bake, covered, at 350°F for 30 minutes or until heated through. Top with remaining ⅔ *cup* onions; bake, uncovered, 5 minutes or until onions are golden brown.

Makes 4 servings

49

Cheesy Broccoli 'n Mushroom Bake

2 packages (10 ounces each) frozen broccoli spears, thawed

1 can (10¾ ounces) condensed cream of mushroom soup

½ cup **MIRACLE WHIP**® Salad Dressing

½ cup milk

1 cup **KRAFT**® Shredded Cheddar Cheese

½ cup coarsely crushed croutons

• ARRANGE broccoli in 12×8-inch baking dish.

• WHISK together soup, salad dressing and milk. Pour over broccoli. Sprinkle with cheese and croutons.

• BAKE at 350°F for 30 to 35 minutes or until thoroughly heated.   *Makes 6 to 8 servings*

Prep Time: 10 minutes
Bake Time: 35 minutes

Cheesy Broccoli 'n Mushroom Bake

Florentine Chicken

2 boxes (10 ounces each) BIRDS EYE® frozen
  Chopped Spinach
1 package (1.25 ounces) hollandaise sauce mix
½ teaspoon TABASCO® Pepper Sauce or to taste
⅓ cup shredded Cheddar cheese, divided
1½ cups cooked cubed chicken

Preheat oven to 350°F.

Cook spinach according to package directions; drain.
Prepare hollandaise sauce according to package directions.

Blend spinach, hollandaise sauce, Tabasco sauce and half
of cheese. Pour into 9×9-inch baking dish; top with
chicken.

Sprinkle remaining cheese on top. Bake 10 to 12 minutes
or until heated through.   *Makes 4 servings*

Prep Time: 2 minutes
Cook Time: 10 to 12 minutes

Turkey Broccoli Bake

1 bag (16 ounces) frozen broccoli cuts, thawed, drained
2 cups cubed cooked turkey or chicken
2 cups soft bread cubes
8 ounces sliced American cheese, divided
1 jar (12 ounces) HEINZ® HomeStyle Turkey or Chicken Gravy
½ cup undiluted evaporated milk
Dash pepper

In buttered 9-inch square baking dish, layer broccoli, turkey, bread cubes and cheese. Combine gravy, milk and pepper; pour over cheese. Bake in 375°F oven, 40 minutes. Let stand 5 minutes.   *Makes 6 servings*

Spaghetti Bake

1 pound BOB EVANS® Dinner Link Sausage
   (regular or Italian)
1 (8-ounce) can tomato sauce
1 (6-ounce) can tomato paste
1 (4-ounce) can sliced mushrooms, drained
½ teaspoon salt
½ teaspoon dried basil leaves
½ teaspoon dried oregano leaves
6 ounces spaghetti, cooked according to package
   directions and drained
⅓ cup shredded mozzarella cheese
2 tablespoons grated Parmesan cheese
   Fresh basil leaves and tomato slices (optional)

Preheat oven to 375°F. Cut sausage links into bite-size
pieces. Cook in medium skillet over medium heat until
browned, stirring occasionally. Drain off any drippings; set
aside. Combine tomato sauce, tomato paste, mushrooms,
salt, dried basil and oregano in large bowl. Add spaghetti
and reserved sausage; mix well. Spoon into lightly greased
1½-quart casserole dish; sprinkle with cheeses. Bake 20 to
30 minutes or until heated through. Garnish with fresh
basil and tomato slices, if desired. Serve hot. Refrigerate
leftovers. *Makes 4 servings*

Spaghetti Bake

Vegetable Beef Pot Pie

$\frac{1}{3}$ cup all-purpose flour

1 teaspoon salt

$\frac{1}{4}$ teaspoon black pepper

2 pounds lean stewing beef, cut into cubes

$\frac{1}{4}$ Butter Flavor CRISCO® Stick or $\frac{1}{4}$ cup Butter Flavor CRISCO® all-vegetable shortening plus additional for greasing, divided

1 medium onion, finely chopped

2 cups beef broth

$\frac{1}{2}$ cup red cooking wine

2 tablespoons tomato paste or ketchup

2 tablespoons finely chopped parsley

1 teaspoon minced garlic

$\frac{1}{4}$ teaspoon dried thyme leaves

1 package (32 ounces) *or* 1$\frac{1}{2}$ packages (20 ounces each) frozen vegetables for stew

1 (9-inch) Classic CRISCO® Single Crust (recipe page 61)

1 egg, lightly beaten

1. Combine flour, salt and pepper in paper or plastic bag. Add beef, shake until well coated.

2. Melt 3 tablespoons shortening in Dutch oven. Brown beef on all sides in batches. Remove beef with slotted spoon to separate container.

3. Melt remaining 1 tablespoon shortening in Dutch oven. Sauté onion until soft. Add broth, wine, tomato paste, parsley, garlic and thyme. Stir to combine.

4. Return meat to Dutch oven. Bring to a boil. Reduce heat. Simmer, uncovered, 2 to 2½ hours or until meat is tender, stirring occasionally. Add frozen vegetables. Mix to combine. Keep warm.

5. Heat oven to 375°F. Grease 13×9×2-inch pan with shortening.

6. Prepare crust. Press dough between hands to form 5-inch square. Roll dough into 13×9-inch rectangle between sheets of waxed paper. Peel off top sheet.

7. Spoon beef mixture into pan. Flip pastry carefully over filling. Remove other sheet of waxed paper. Tuck in pastry or flute edge. Cut slits in crust for escape of steam. Brush crust with beaten egg.

8. Bake 30 to 45 minutes or until lightly browned. *Do not overbake*. Serve hot. *Makes 8 servings*

Hungarian Goulash Casserole

1 pound ground pork
¼ teaspoon salt
¼ teaspoon pepper
¼ teaspoon ground nutmeg
1 tablespoon vegetable oil
1 cup reduced-fat sour cream, divided
1 tablespoon cornstarch
1 can (10¾ ounces) cream of celery soup
1 cup milk
1 teaspoon sweet Hungarian paprika
1 package (12 ounces) egg noodles, cooked and
    drained
2 teaspoons minced fresh dill (optional)

1. Preheat oven to 325°F. Spray 13×9-inch casserole dish with nonstick cooking spray.

2. Combine pork, salt, pepper and nutmeg in bowl. Shape into 1-inch meatballs. Heat oil in large skillet over medium-high heat. Add meatballs. Cook 10 minutes or until browned on all sides and no longer pink in the center. Remove meatballs from skillet; discard drippings.

3. Stir together ¼ cup sour cream and cornstarch in small bowl. Spoon into same skillet. Add remaining ¾ cup sour cream, soup, milk and paprika. Stir until smooth.

4. Spoon cooked noodles into prepared dish. Arrange meatballs over noodles and cover with sauce. Bake 20 minutes or until hot. Sprinkle with dill if desired.

Make 4 to 6 servings

Hungarian Goulash Casserole

Delicious Ground Beef Medley

1 pound ground beef
$\frac{1}{2}$ cup chopped onion
$\frac{1}{4}$ cup chopped celery
2 cups uncooked elbow macaroni
1 can ($10\frac{3}{4}$ ounces) condensed cream of
    chicken soup
1 can ($10\frac{3}{4}$ ounces) condensed cream of
    mushroom soup
$\frac{2}{3}$ cup milk
$\frac{1}{2}$ teaspoon salt
    Dash of pepper
$\frac{1}{2}$ cup chopped green bell pepper
1 can (16 ounces) whole kernel corn, drained

1. Brown ground beef with onion and celery, stirring to break up meat. Drain.

2. Cook macaroni according to package directions. Drain.

3. In $2\frac{1}{2}$-quart casserole dish, combine soups with milk, salt and pepper. Add ground beef, macaroni, green pepper and corn. Bake at 350°F for 30 minutes.

Makes 8 servings

Favorite recipe from **North Dakota Beef Commission**

Classic Crisco® Single Crust

1⅓ cups all-purpose flour
½ teaspoon salt
½ CRISCO® Stick or ½ cup CRISCO® Shortening
3 tablespoons cold water

1. Spoon flour into measuring cup and level. Combine flour and salt in medium bowl.

2. Cut in ½ cup shortening using pastry blender or 2 knives until all flour is blended to form pea-size chunks.

3. Sprinkle with water, 1 tablespoon at a time. Toss lightly with fork until dough forms a ball.

4. Press dough between hands to form 5- to 6-inch "pancake." Flour rolling surface and rolling pin lightly. Roll dough into circle. Trim 1 inch larger than upside-down pie plate. Loosen dough carefully.

5. Fold dough into quarters. Unfold and press into pie plate. Fold edge under. Flute.

Makes 8- to 9-inch single crust

Broccoli and Beef Pasta

1 pound lean ground beef

2 cloves garlic, minced

1 can (about 14 ounces) beef broth

1 medium onion, thinly sliced

1 cup uncooked rotini pasta

½ teaspoon dried basil leaves

½ teaspoon dried oregano leaves

½ teaspoon dried thyme leaves

1 can (15 ounces) Italian-style tomatoes, undrained

2 cups broccoli florets *or* 1 package (10 ounces) frozen broccoli, thawed

3 ounces shredded Cheddar cheese or grated Parmesan cheese

1. Combine meat and garlic in large nonstick skillet; cook over high heat until meat is no longer pink, breaking meat apart. Pour off drippings. Place meat in large bowl; set aside.

2. Add broth, onion, pasta, basil, oregano and thyme to skillet. Bring to a boil. Reduce heat to medium-high and boil 10 minutes; add tomatoes with juice. Increase heat to high and bring to a boil; stir in broccoli. Cook, uncovered, 6 to 8 minutes, stirring occasionally, until broccoli is crisp-tender and pasta is tender. Drain excess liquid. Add pasta mixture to beef; mix well.

3. Spoon mixture into well-greased 9-inch baking dish. Bake, uncovered, at 350°F for 20 minutes or until hot.

Makes 4 servings

Broccoli and Beef Pasta

Pork Chops O'Brien

1 tablespoon vegetable oil
6 pork chops, ½ to ¾ inch thick
    Seasoned salt
1 can (10¾ ounces) condensed cream of celery soup
½ cup milk
½ cup sour cream
¼ teaspoon pepper
1 bag (24 ounces) frozen O'Brien or hash brown
    potatoes, thawed
1 cup (4 ounces) shredded Cheddar cheese, divided
1⅓ cups *French's*® French Fried Onions, divided

Preheat oven to 350°F. In large skillet, heat oil. Brown
pork chops on both sides; drain. Sprinkle chops with
seasoned salt; set aside. In large bowl, combine soup, milk,
sour cream, pepper and ½ teaspoon seasoned salt. Stir in
potatoes, ½ cup cheese and ⅔ *cup* French Fried Onions.
Spoon mixture into 13×9-inch baking dish; arrange pork
chops on top. Bake, covered, at 350°F for 35 to 40 minutes
or until pork chops are done. Top chops with remaining
½ cup cheese and ⅔ *cup* onions; bake, uncovered,
5 minutes or until onions are golden brown.

Makes 6 servings

Microwave Directions: Omit oil. Prepare soup-potato
mixture as above; spoon into 12×8-inch microwave-safe
dish. Cook, covered, on HIGH 5 minutes. Stir well.
Arrange unbrowned pork chops on top with meatiest
parts toward edges of dish. Cook, covered, on MEDIUM
(50-60%) 15 minutes. Turn chops over; sprinkle with
seasoned salt. Stir potatoes and rotate dish.

Cook, covered, on MEDIUM 12 to 15 minutes or until pork chops are done. Top chops with remaining cheese and ⅔ *cup* onions; cook, uncovered, on HIGH 1 minute or until cheese melts. Let stand 5 minutes.

Grandma's Tip

A casserole refers to both a specific baking utensil and the food it contains. A casserole dish is a deep round, oval, square or rectangle ovenproof container often with two short handles. It may or may not be covered. Casseroles are usually made of glass, earthenware or porcelain. They are measured by their volume in quarts. The most common sizes are 1, 1½, 2, 2½ and 3 quarts.

Reuben Noodle Bake

8 ounces uncooked egg noodles

5 ounces thinly sliced deli-style corned beef

1 can (14½ ounces) sauerkraut with caraway seeds, drained

2 cups (8 ounces) shredded Swiss cheese

½ cup Thousand Island dressing

½ cup milk

1 tablespoon prepared mustard

2 slices pumpernickel bread

1 tablespoon butter, melted

1. Preheat oven to 350°F. Spray 13×9-inch baking dish with nonstick cooking spray.

2. Cook noodles according to package directions until al dente. Drain.

3. Meanwhile, cut corned beef into bite-size pieces. Combine noodles, corned beef, sauerkraut and cheese in large bowl. Spread in prepared dish.

4. Combine dressing, milk and mustard in small bowl. Spoon dressing mixture evenly over noodle mixture.

5. Tear bread into large pieces. Process in food processor or blender until crumbs form. Combine bread crumbs and margarine in small bowl; sprinkle evenly over casserole. Bake, uncovered, 25 to 30 minutes or until heated through. *Makes 6 servings*

Reuben Noodle Bake

Spaghetti Rolls

1 package (8 ounces) manicotti shells
2 pounds ground beef
1 tablespoon onion powder
1 teaspoon salt
½ teaspoon black pepper
2 cups spaghetti sauce, divided
1 cup (4 ounces) shredded pizza-flavored cheese
   blend or mozzarella cheese

1. Cook pasta according to package directions. Place in colander, then rinse under warm running water. Drain well.

2. Preheat oven to 350°F. Grease 13×9-inch baking pan.

3. Brown beef in large skillet over medium-high heat, stirring to separate meat; drain drippings. Stir in onion powder, salt and pepper. Stir in 1 cup spaghetti sauce; cool and set aside.

4. Reserve ½ cup ground beef mixture. Combine remaining beef mixture with cheese in large bowl. Fill shells with remaining beef mixture using spoon.

5. Arrange shells in prepared pan. Combine remaining 1 cup spaghetti sauce with reserved beef mixture in small bowl; blend well. Pour over shells. Cover with foil.

6. Bake 20 to 30 minutes or until hot. Garnish as desired.

Makes 4 servings

Spaghetti Rolls

Maple Link Sweet Potatoes and Apples

4 medium to large sweet potatoes
2 Granny Smith or other tart apples
1 (12-ounce) package BOB EVANS® Maple Links
½ teaspoon salt
¾ cup packed brown sugar, divided
¼ teaspoon ground nutmeg
¼ teaspoon ground cinnamon
¼ cup butter or margarine
1 cup apple juice

Cook unpeeled potatoes in 4 quarts boiling water 15 minutes. Drain and cool slightly. Peel and cut into ¼-inch slices. Peel, core and cut apples into ¼-inch slices. Preheat oven to 350°F. Cook sausage in large skillet until browned. Drain off any drippings; place on paper towels. Cut each sausage link into 3 pieces. Arrange potatoes, apples and sausage alternately in buttered 13×9-inch (or similar size) baking dish. Sprinkle with salt, ½ cup brown sugar, nutmeg and cinnamon. Dot with butter. Pour apple juice over top. Cover and bake 30 minutes. Remove from oven; sprinkle with remaining ¼ cup brown sugar. Bake, uncovered, 25 to 30 minutes more or until lightly browned and potatoes are tender. Refrigerate leftovers.

Makes 8 servings

Chili Cornbread Casserole

1 pound ground beef
1 medium onion, chopped
1 jar (16 ounces) RAGÚ® Cheese Creations!®
  Double Cheddar Sauce
1 can (19 ounces) red kidney beans, rinsed and
  drained
1 can (8¾ ounces) whole kernel corn, drained
2 to 3 teaspoons chili powder
1 package (12 ounces) cornbread mix

Preheat oven to 400°F. In 12-inch skillet, brown ground
beef and onion over medium-high heat; drain. Stir in
Ragú Cheese Creations! Sauce, beans, corn and chili
powder.

Meanwhile, prepare cornbread mix according to package
directions. Do not bake.

In ungreased 2-quart baking dish, spread ground beef
mixture. Top with cornbread mixture. Bake, uncovered,
20 minutes or until toothpick inserted into center of
cornbread comes out clean and top is golden.

Makes 6 servings

Prep Time: 10 minutes
Cook Time: 20 minutes

Smoked Sausage and Sauerkraut Casserole

6 fully-cooked smoked sausage links, such as German or Polish sausage (about 1½ pounds)

⅓ cup water

¼ cup packed brown sugar

2 tablespoons country-style Dijon mustard, Dijon mustard or German-style mustard

1 teaspoon caraway seed

½ teaspoon dill weed

1 jar (32 ounces) sauerkraut, drained

1 small green bell pepper, stemmed, seeded and diced

½ cup (2 ounces) shredded Swiss cheese

1. Place sausage in large skillet with water. Cover; bring to a boil over medium heat. Reduce heat to low; simmer, covered, 10 minutes. Uncover and simmer until water evaporates and sausages brown lightly.

2. While sausage is cooking, combine sugar, mustard, caraway and dill in medium saucepan; stir until blended. Add sauerkraut and bell pepper; stir until well mixed. Cook, covered, over medium heat 10 minutes or until very hot.

3. Spoon sauerkraut into microwavable 2- to 3-quart casserole; sprinkle with cheese. Place sausage over sauerkraut; cover. Microwave at HIGH 30 seconds or until cheese melts.   *Makes 6 servings*

Prep and Cook Time: 20 minutes

Smoked Sausage and Sauerkraut Casserole

Shepherd's Pie

1⅓ cups instant mashed potato buds
1⅔ cups milk
  2 tablespoons margarine or butter
  1 teaspoon salt, divided
  1 pound ground beef
¼ teaspoon black pepper
  1 jar (12 ounces) beef gravy
  1 package (10 ounces) frozen mixed vegetables,
    thawed and drained
¾ cup grated Parmesan cheese

1. Preheat broiler. Prepare 4 servings of mashed potatoes according to package directions using milk, margarine and ½ teaspoon salt.

2. While mashed potatoes are cooking, brown meat in medium broilerproof skillet over medium-high heat, stirring to separate meat. Drain drippings. Sprinkle meat with remaining ½ teaspoon salt and pepper. Add gravy and vegetables; mix well. Cook over medium-low heat 5 minutes or until hot.

3. Spoon prepared potatoes around outside edge of skillet, leaving 3-inch circle in center. Sprinkle cheese evenly over potatoes. Broil 4 to 5 inches from heat source 3 minutes or until cheese is golden brown and meat mixture is bubbly. *Makes 4 servings*

Prep and Cook Time: 28 minutes

Shepherd's Pie

Johnnie Marzetti

1 tablespoon CRISCO® Oil*

1 cup chopped celery

1 cup chopped onion

1 medium green bell pepper, chopped

1 pound ground beef round

1 can (14½ ounces) Italian-style stewed tomatoes, undrained

1 can (8 ounces) tomato sauce

1 can (6 ounces) tomato paste

1 cup water

1 bay leaf

1½ teaspoons dried basil leaves

1¼ teaspoons salt

¼ teaspoon black pepper

1 package (12 ounces) egg noodles, cooked and well drained

½ cup plain dry bread crumbs

1 cup (4 ounces) shredded sharp Cheddar cheese

Use your favorite Crisco Oil product.

1. Heat oven to 375°F. Oil 12½×8½×2-inch baking dish lightly. Place cooling rack on countertop.

2. Heat one tablespoon oil in large skillet on medium heat. Add celery, onion and green pepper. Cook and stir until tender. Remove vegetables from skillet. Set aside.

continued on page 78

Johnnie Marzetti

Johnnie Marzetti, *continued*

Add meat to skillet. Cook until browned, stirring occasionally. Return vegetables to skillet. Add tomatoes, tomato sauce, tomato paste, water, bay leaf, basil, salt and black pepper. Reduce heat to low. Simmer 5 minutes, stirring occasionally. Remove bay leaf.

3. Place noodles in baking dish. Spoon meat mixture over noodles. Sprinkle with bread crumbs and cheese.

4. Bake at 375°F for 15 to 20 minutes or until cheese melts. *Do not overbake.* Remove baking dish to cooling rack. Garnish, if desired.   *Makes 8 servings*

Grandma's Tip

When reheating a frozen casserole, it is best to thaw the casserole in the refrigerator overnight. If a casserole is not thawed in the refrigerator, cover and reheat in a 350°F oven for almost double the cooking time.

Savory Pork Chop Supper

6 medium potatoes, thinly sliced (about 5 cups)
1⅓ cups *French's*® French Fried Onions, divided
1 jar (2 ounces) sliced mushrooms, drained
2 tablespoons butter or margarine
¼ cup soy sauce
1½ teaspoons ground mustard
½ teaspoon *Frank's*® *RedHot*® Cayenne Pepper Sauce
⅛ teaspoon garlic powder
1 tablespoon vegetable oil
6 pork chops, ½ to ¾ inch thick

Preheat oven to 350°F. In 12×8-inch baking dish, layer
half the potatoes and ⅔ *cup* French Fried Onions. Top
with mushrooms and remaining potatoes. In small
saucepan, melt butter; stir in soy sauce, mustard, **Frank's**
RedHot Sauce and garlic powder. Brush half the soy sauce
mixture over potatoes. In large skillet, heat oil. Brown
pork chops on both sides; drain. Arrange chops over
potatoes and brush with remaining soy sauce mixture.
Bake, covered, at 350°F for 1 hour. Bake, uncovered,
15 minutes or until pork chops and potatoes are done. Top
chops with remaining ⅔ *cup* onions; bake, uncovered,
5 minutes or until onions are golden brown.

Makes 4 to 6 servings

Chili Spaghetti Casserole

8 ounces uncooked spaghetti

1 pound lean ground beef

1 medium onion, chopped

¼ teaspoon salt

⅛ teaspoon black pepper

1 can (15 ounces) vegetarian chili with beans

1 can (14½ ounces) Italian-style stewed tomatoes, undrained

1½ cups (6 ounces) shredded sharp Cheddar cheese, divided

½ cup reduced-fat sour cream

1½ teaspoons chili powder

¼ teaspoon garlic powder

1. Preheat oven to 350°F. Spray 13×9-inch baking dish with nonstick cooking spray.

2. Cook pasta according to package directions until al dente. Drain and place in prepared dish.

3. Meanwhile, place beef and onion in large skillet; season with salt and pepper. Brown beef over medium-high heat until beef is no longer pink, stirring to separate meat. Drain fat. Stir in chili, tomatoes with juice, 1 cup cheese, sour cream, chili powder and garlic powder.

4. Add chili mixture to pasta; stir until pasta is well coated. Sprinkle with remaining ½ cup cheese.

5. Cover tightly with foil and bake 30 minutes or until hot and bubbly. Let stand 5 minutes before serving.

Makes 8 servings

Chili Spaghetti Casserole

Polish Reuben Casserole

2 cans (10¾ ounces each) condensed cream of
    mushroom soup
1⅓ cups milk
 ½ cup chopped onion
 1 tablespoon prepared mustard
 2 cans (16 ounces each) sauerkraut, rinsed and
    drained
 1 package (8 ounces) uncooked medium-width
    noodles
1½ pounds Polish sausage, cut into ½-inch pieces
 2 cups (8 ounces) shredded Swiss cheese
 ¾ cup whole wheat bread crumbs
 2 tablespoons butter, melted

1. Combine soup, milk, onion and mustard in medium
bowl; blend well. Spread sauerkraut into greased
13×9-inch pan. Top with uncooked noodles. Spoon soup
mixture evenly over noodles; cover with sausage. Top with
cheese. Combine bread crumbs and butter in small bowl;
sprinkle over casserole.

2. Cover pan tightly with foil. Bake in preheated 350°F
oven 1 hour or until noodles are tender. Garnish as
desired. *Makes 8 to 10 servings*

Polish Reuben Casserole

Oven-Easy Beef

4 cups frozen hash brown potatoes, thawed

3 tablespoons vegetable oil

⅛ teaspoon black pepper

1 pound ground beef

1 cup water

1 package (about ¾ ounce) brown gravy mix

½ teaspoon garlic salt

1 package (10 ounces) frozen mixed vegetables,
  thawed and drained

1 cup (4 ounces) shredded Cheddar cheese, divided

1⅓ cups *French's*® French Fried Onions, divided

Preheat oven to 400°F. In 12×8-inch baking dish, combine potatoes, oil and pepper. Firmly press potato mixture evenly across bottom and up sides of dish to form a shell. Bake, uncovered, at 400°F for 15 minutes. Meanwhile, in large skillet, brown ground beef; drain. Stir in water, gravy mix and garlic salt; bring to a boil. Add mixed vegetables; reduce heat to medium and cook, uncovered, 5 minutes. Remove from heat and stir in ½ cup cheese and ⅔ cup French Fried Onions; spoon into hot potato shell. *Reduce oven temperature to 350°F.* Bake, uncovered, at 350°F for 15 minutes or until heated through. Top with remaining ½ cup cheese and ⅔ cup onions; bake, uncovered, 5 minutes or until onions are golden brown.   *Makes 4 to 6 servings*

Spinach-Potato Bake

1 pound extra-lean (90% lean) ground beef

½ cup sliced fresh mushrooms

1 small onion, chopped

2 cloves garlic, minced

1 package (10 ounces) frozen chopped spinach,
   thawed, well drained

½ teaspoon ground nutmeg

1 pound russet potatoes, peeled, cooked and mashed

¼ cup light sour cream

¼ cup fat-free (skim) milk

   Salt and black pepper

½ cup (2 ounces) shredded Cheddar cheese

1. Preheat oven to 400°F. Spray deep 9-inch casserole
dish with nonstick cooking spray.

2. Brown ground beef in large skillet, stirring to break up
meat; drain. Add mushrooms, onion and garlic; cook until
tender. Stir in spinach and nutmeg; cover. Heat
thoroughly, stirring occasionally.

3. Combine potatoes, sour cream and milk. Add to
ground beef mixture; season with salt and pepper to taste.
Spoon into prepared casserole dish; sprinkle with cheese.

4. Bake 15 to 20 minutes or until slightly puffed and
cheese is melted. *Makes 6 servings*

Apple, Bean and Ham Casserole

1 pound boneless ham

3 cans (15 ounces each) Great Northern beans, drained and rinsed

1 small onion, diced

1 medium Granny Smith apple, diced

3 tablespoons dark molasses

3 tablespoons packed brown sugar

1 tablespoon Dijon mustard

1 teaspoon ground allspice

¼ cup thinly sliced green onions *or* 1 tablespoon chopped fresh parsley

1. Preheat oven to 350°F. Cut ham into 1-inch cubes. Combine ham, beans, onion, apple, molasses, brown sugar, mustard and allspice in 3-quart casserole; mix well. Cover; bake 45 minutes or until most liquid is absorbed. Cool casserole completely. Cover and refrigerate up to 2 days.

2. To complete recipe, stir ⅓ cup water into casserole. Microwave at HIGH 10 minutes or until hot and bubbly. Or, heat in preheated 350°F oven 40 minutes or until hot and bubbly. Sprinkle with green onions before serving.

Makes 6 servings

Make-Ahead Time: up to 2 days in refrigerator
Final Cook Time: 15 minutes

Apple, Bean and Ham Casserole

Ham & Macaroni Twists

2 cups rotini or elbow macaroni, cooked in unsalted
    water and drained
1½ cups (8 ounces) cubed cooked ham
1⅓ cups *French's®* French Fried Onions, divided
    1 package (10 ounces) frozen broccoli spears,*
        thawed and drained
    1 cup milk
    1 can (10¾ ounces) condensed cream of celery soup
    1 cup (4 ounces) shredded Cheddar cheese, divided
    ¼ teaspoon garlic powder
    ¼ teaspoon pepper

*1 small head fresh broccoli (about ½ pound) may be substituted for frozen
spears. Divide into spears and cook 3 to 4 minutes before using.*

Preheat oven to 350°F. In 12×8-inch baking dish,
combine hot macaroni, ham and ⅔ *cup* French Fried
Onions. Divide broccoli spears into 6 small bunches.
Arrange bunches of spears down center of dish,
alternating direction of flowerets. In small bowl, combine
milk, soup, ½ cup cheese and the seasonings; pour over
casserole. Bake, covered, at 350°F for 30 minutes or until
heated through. Top with remaining ½ cup cheese and
sprinkle remaining ⅔ *cup* onions down center; bake,
uncovered, 5 minutes or until onions are golden brown.

Makes 4 to 6 servings

Microwave Directions: In 12×8-inch microwave-safe dish, prepare macaroni mixture and arrange broccoli spears as above. Prepare soup mixture as above; pour over casserole. Cook, covered, on HIGH 8 minutes or until broccoli is done. Rotate dish halfway through cooking time. Top with remaining cheese and onions as above; cook, uncovered, 1 minute or until cheese melts. Let stand 5 minutes.

Easy Oven Beef Stew

2 pounds boneless beef stew meat, cut into
1½-inch cubes

1 can (16 ounces) tomatoes, undrained, cut up

1 can (10½ ounces) condensed beef broth

1 cup HOLLAND HOUSE® Red Cooking Wine

1 tablespoon dried Italian seasonings*

6 potatoes, peeled, quartered

6 carrots, cut into 2-inch pieces

3 ribs celery, cut into 1-inch pieces

2 medium onions, peeled, quartered

⅓ cup instant tapioca

¼ teaspoon black pepper

Chopped fresh parsley

You can substitute 1½ teaspoons each of dried basil and oregano for Italian seasonings.

Heat oven to 325°F. Combine all ingredients except parsley in ovenproof Dutch oven; cover. Bake 2½ to 3 hours or until meat and vegetables are tender. Garnish with parsley.   *Makes 8 servings*

Turkey and Stuffing Bake

- 1 jar (4½ ounces) sliced mushrooms
- ¼ cup butter or margarine
- ½ cup diced celery
- ½ cup chopped onion
- 1¼ cups HIDDEN VALLEY® The Original Ranch® Dressing, divided
- ⅔ cup water
- 3 cups seasoned stuffing mix
- ⅓ cup sweetened dried cranberries
- 3 cups coarsely shredded cooked turkey (about 1 pound)

Drain mushrooms, reserving liquid; set aside. Melt butter over medium high heat in a large skillet. Add celery and onion; sauté for 4 minutes or until soft. Remove from heat and stir in ½ cup dressing, water and reserved mushroom liquid. Stir in stuffing mix and cranberries until thoroughly moistened. Combine turkey, mushrooms and remaining ¾ cup dressing in a separate bowl; spread evenly in a greased 8-inch baking dish. Top with stuffing mixture. Bake at 350°F. for 40 minutes or until bubbly and brown. *Makes 4 to 6 servings*

Turkey and Stuffing Bake

Chicken Dijon & Pasta

1 (3- to 4-pound) chicken, cut-up and skinned, if
   desired
⅓ cup *French's®* Napa Valley Style Dijon Mustard
⅓ cup Italian salad dressing
1 can (10¾ ounces) condensed cream of
   chicken soup
4 cups hot cooked rotini pasta (8 ounces uncooked)
1⅓ cups *French's®* French Fried Onions, divided
1 cup diced tomatoes
1 cup diced zucchini
2 tablespoons minced parsley or basil leaves
   (optional)

1. Preheat oven to 400°F. Place chicken in shallow
roasting pan. Mix mustard and dressing. Spoon half of
mixture over chicken. Bake, uncovered, 40 minutes.

2. Combine soup, *½ cup water* and remaining mustard
mixture. Toss pasta with sauce, *⅔ cup* French Fried
Onions, vegetables and parsley. Spoon mixture around
chicken.

3. Bake, uncovered, 15 minutes or until chicken is no
longer pink in center. Sprinkle with remaining ⅔ cup
onions. Bake 1 minute or until onions are golden.

Makes 6 servings

Prep Time: 15 minutes
Cook Time: about 1 hour

Chicken Dijon & Pasta

Turkey Tetrazzini

1¼ cups skim milk
¾ cup turkey broth or chicken bouillon
2 tablespoons cornstarch
½ teaspoon salt
½ teaspoon garlic powder
⅛ teaspoon pepper
¼ cup grated Parmesan cheese
2 tablespoons dry white wine
1 can (4 ounces) mushrooms, drained
1 jar (2 ounces) chopped pimiento, drained
4 ounces spaghetti, cooked according to package
   instructions and drained
2 cups cooked turkey, cut into ½-inch cubes
2 tablespoons sliced almonds

1. Preheat oven to 375°F.

2. In 3-quart saucepan, over medium heat, combine milk, broth, cornstarch, salt, garlic powder and pepper. Bring mixture to boil, stirring constantly. Remove from heat and stir in cheese, wine, mushrooms, pimiento, spaghetti and turkey.

3. Pour turkey mixture into lightly greased 9-inch square casserole dish. Top with almonds. Bake 25 minutes or until mixture bubbles and top is browned.

Makes 4 servings

Favorite recipe from **National Turkey Federation**

Chicken à la King Express

3 boneless skinless chicken breasts, cooked and
  diced
1 can (10¾ ounces) reduced-fat condensed cream of
  celery soup
½ cup sliced green onions
½ cup sliced mushrooms
2 tablespoons low-fat (1%) milk
1 clove garlic, minced
½ teaspoon salt
¼ teaspoon white pepper
2 English muffins, halved

1. Preheat oven to 450°F. Combine chicken, soup, green
onions, mushrooms, milk, garlic, salt and pepper in
medium bowl; mix well. Spray 4 (6-ounce) custard cups
with nonstick cooking spray; place equal portions of
chicken mixture in each cup. Top with English muffin
halves, split sides down.

2. Place custard cups on baking sheet; bake 13 to
15 minutes or until muffins are golden brown and chicken
mixture is hot and bubbly. Invert custard cups onto
serving dishes. *Makes 4 servings*

Lighter Stuffed Peppers

1 can (10¾ ounces) reduced-fat condensed tomato
   soup, divided

¼ cup water

8 ounces extra-lean ground turkey

1 cup cooked rice

¾ cup frozen corn, thawed

¼ cup each sliced celery

¼ cup chopped red bell pepper

1 teaspoon dried Italian seasoning

½ teaspoon hot pepper sauce

2 green, yellow or red bell peppers, cut in half
   lengthwise, seeds removed

1. Blend ¼ cup soup and water in small bowl. Pour into
8×8-inch baking dish; set aside. Brown turkey in large
skillet over medium-high heat; drain well. Combine
remaining soup with cooked turkey, rice, corn, celery,
chopped pepper, Italian seasoning and hot pepper sauce
in large bowl; mix well.

2. Fill pepper halves equally with turkey mixture. Place
stuffed peppers on top of soup mixture in baking dish.
Cover and bake at 350°F 35 to 40 minutes. Place peppers
on serving dish and spoon remaining sauce from baking
dish over peppers. *Makes 4 servings*

Lighter Stuffed Peppers

Chicken Normandy Style

2 tablespoons butter, divided

3 cups peeled, thinly sliced sweet apples, such as Fuji or Braeburn (about 3 apples)

1 pound ground chicken

¼ cup apple brandy or apple juice

1 can (10¾ ounces) cream of chicken soup

¼ cup finely chopped green onion, green part only

2 teaspoons fresh minced sage *or* ½ teaspoon dried sage

¼ teaspoon pepper

1 package (12 ounces) egg noodles, cooked and drained

1. Preheat oven to 350°F.

2. Melt 1 tablespoon butter in 12-inch nonstick skillet. Add apple slices and cook and stir over medium heat 7 to 10 minutes or until tender; remove apple slices from skillet.

3. Add ground chicken to same skillet; cook and stir over medium heat until brown, breaking up with spoon. Stir in apple brandy and cook 2 minutes. Stir in soup, green onion, sage, pepper and apple slices. Simmer 5 minutes.

4. Toss noodles with remaining 1 tablespoon butter. Spoon into well-greased 9-inch square pan. Top with chicken mixture. Bake for 15 minutes or until hot.

Makes 4 servings

Chicken Normandy Style

Turkey Vegetable Crescent Pie

2 cans (about 14 ounces) fat-free reduced-sodium
chicken broth

1 medium onion, diced

1¼ pounds turkey tenderloins, cut into ¾-inch pieces

3 cups diced red potatoes

1 teaspoon chopped fresh rosemary *or* ½ teaspoon
dried rosemary

¼ teaspoon salt

⅛ teaspoon black pepper

1 bag (16 ounces) frozen mixed vegetables

1 bag (10 ounces) frozen mixed vegetables

⅓ cup fat-free (skim) milk plus additional, if
necessary

3 tablespoons cornstarch

1 package (8 ounces) refrigerated reduced-fat
crescent rolls

1. Bring broth to a boil in large saucepan. Add onion;
reduce heat and simmer 3 minutes. Add turkey; return to a
boil. Reduce heat, cover and simmer 7 to 9 minutes or
until turkey is no longer pink. Remove turkey from
saucepan with slotted spoon; place in 13×9-inch baking
dish.

continued on page 102

Turkey Vegetable Crescent Pie

Turkey Vegetable Crescent Pie, continued

2. Return broth to a boil. Add potatoes, rosemary, salt and pepper; simmer 2 minutes. Return to a boil and stir in mixed vegetables. Simmer, covered, 7 to 8 minutes or until potatoes are tender. Remove vegetables with slotted spoon. Drain in colander set over bowl; reserve broth. Transfer vegetables to baking dish with turkey.

3. Preheat oven to 375°F. Blend ⅓ cup milk with cornstarch in small bowl until smooth. Add enough milk to reserved broth to equal 3 cups. Heat in large saucepan over medium-high heat; whisk in cornstarch mixture, stirring constantly until mixture comes to a boil. Boil 1 minute; remove from heat. Pour over turkey-vegetable mixture in baking dish.

4. Roll out crescent roll dough and separate at perforations; arrange dough pieces decoratively over top of turkey-vegetable mixture. Bake 13 to 15 minutes or until crust is golden brown. *Makes 8 servings*

Chicken-Potato Pot Pie

2 cans (14½ ounces each) chicken broth
1 bay leaf
½ teaspoon white pepper
2 cups cubed Colorado potatoes
1 package (16 ounces) frozen mixed vegetables
1 rib celery, chopped
3 tablespoons butter or margarine
3 tablespoons all-purpose flour
3 cups cubed cooked chicken
4 hard-cooked eggs, sliced
    Pastry for 9-inch pie

Combine broth, bay leaf and pepper in large Dutch oven; bring to a boil. Add potatoes; cover. Reduce heat to medium and cook 5 minutes. Add frozen vegetables and celery; return to a boil. Cover; reduce heat and simmer 8 to 12 minutes. Remove bay leaf. Drain vegetables, reserving broth. Melt butter in Dutch oven over medium heat; add flour, stirring until smooth. Cook 1 minute, stirring constantly. Gradually add reserved broth; cook, stirring constantly, until mixture is thickened and bubbly. Stir in vegetables, chicken and eggs; spoon mixture into round 2½-quart casserole. Roll out pastry; place over chicken mixture. Trim edges; seal and flute. Roll out dough scraps and cut into decorative shapes, if desired. Dampen pastry cutouts with water and arrange over pastry top. Cut slits in pastry to allow steam to escape. Bake at 400°F for 20 minutes or until golden brown.

Makes 6 to 8 servings

Favorite recipe from **Colorado Potato Administrative Committee**

Chicken & Biscuits

¼ cup butter or margarine

4 boneless skinless chicken breasts (about
    1¼ pounds), cut into ½-inch pieces

½ cup chopped onion

½ teaspoon dried thyme leaves

½ teaspoon paprika

¼ teaspoon black pepper

1 can (about 14 ounces) chicken broth, divided

⅓ cup all-purpose flour

1 package (10 ounces) frozen peas and carrots

1 can (12 ounces) refrigerated biscuits

1. Preheat oven to 375°F. Melt butter in large skillet over medium heat. Add chicken, onion, thyme, paprika and pepper. Cook 5 minutes or until chicken is browned.

2. Combine ¼ cup chicken broth with flour; stir until smooth. Set aside.

3. Add remaining chicken broth to skillet; bring to a boil. Gradually add flour mixture, stirring constantly to prevent lumps from forming. Simmer 5 minutes. Add peas and carrots; continue cooking 2 minutes.

4. Transfer to 1½-quart casserole; top with biscuits. Bake 25 to 30 minutes or until biscuits are golden brown.

Makes 4 to 6 servings

Tip: Use an ovenproof skillet to cook chicken and omit the 1½-quart casserole. Place biscuits directly on chicken and vegetable mixture and bake as directed.

Chicken & Biscuits

Zesty Turkey Pot Pie

1 tablespoon vegetable oil

1 small onion, finely chopped

1 jalapeño pepper,* cored, seeded and minced

1 pound ground turkey

½ teaspoon dried thyme leaves

½ teaspoon pepper

1 package (16 ounces) frozen mixed vegetables

2 cans (10¾ ounces each) golden mushroom soup

1 package (11 ounces) refrigerated breadsticks
    (12 breadsticks)

Jalapeño peppers can sting and irritate the skin; wear rubber gloves when handling peppers and do not touch eyes. Wash hands after handling peppers.

1. Preheat oven to 350°F.

2. Heat oil in large skillet. Add onion and jalapeño and sauté over medium heat 5 minutes. Stir in turkey and break up with a spoon. Brown turkey. Stir in thyme, pepper and vegetables. Cook for 5 minutes to thaw. Stir in soup. Cook over medium heat 5 minutes or until piping hot.

3. Spoon turkey mixture into greased 13×9-inch casserole. Pull and stretch breadsticks to lengthen, pressing ends together if necessary to reach across baking dish. Arrange stretched breadsticks in a lattice pattern over turkey, trimming ends. Bake for 15 to 20 minutes or until breadsticks are golden. *Makes 6 servings*

Note: If mixture isn't hot when spooned into casserole, breadsticks may be gummy on the bottom.

Zesty Turkey Pot Pie

Chicken Tetrazzini

8 ounces uncooked spaghetti, broken in half
3 tablespoons butter, divided
¼ cup all-purpose flour
1 teaspoon salt
½ teaspoon paprika
½ teaspoon celery salt
⅛ teaspoon pepper
2 cups milk
1 cup chicken broth
3 cups chopped cooked chicken
1 can (4 ounces) mushrooms, drained
¼ cup pimiento strips
¾ cup (3 ounces) grated Wisconsin Parmesan cheese,
   divided

In large saucepan, cook spaghetti according to package
directions; drain. Return to same saucepan; add
1 tablespoon butter. Stir until melted. Set aside. In 3-quart
saucepan, melt remaining 2 tablespoons butter over
medium heat; stir in flour, salt, paprika, celery salt and
pepper. Remove from heat; gradually stir in milk and
chicken broth. Cook over medium heat, stirring
constantly, until thickened. Add chicken, mushrooms,
pimiento, spaghetti and ¼ cup cheese; heat thoroughly.
Place chicken mixture on ovenproof platter or in shallow
casserole; sprinkle remaining ½ cup cheese over top. Broil
about 3 inches from heat until lightly browned.

Makes 6 to 8 servings

Favorite recipe from **Wisconsin Milk Marketing Board**

Homespun
Turkey 'n' Vegetables

1 package (9 ounces) frozen cut green beans, thawed
    and drained
1 can (14 ounces) sliced carrots, drained
1⅓ cups *French's*® French Fried Onions, divided
1 can (16 ounces) whole potatoes, drained
1 can (10¾ ounces) condensed cream of celery soup
¼ cup milk
1 tablespoon *French's*® Classic Yellow® Mustard
¼ teaspoon garlic powder
1 pound uncooked turkey breast slices

Preheat oven to 375°F. In 12×8-inch baking dish,
combine green beans, carrots and ⅔ *cup* French Fried
Onions. Slice potatoes into halves; arrange as many halves
as will fit, cut side down, around edges of baking dish.
Combine any remaining potatoes with vegetables in dish.
In medium bowl, combine soup, milk, mustard and garlic
powder; pour half the soup mixture over vegetables.
Overlap turkey slices on vegetables. Pour remaining soup
mixture over turkey and potatoes. Bake, covered, at 375°F
for 40 minutes or until turkey is done. Top turkey with
remaining ⅔ *cup* onions; bake, uncovered, 3 minutes or
until onions are golden brown.   *Makes 4 servings*

Chicken Pot Pie

2 teaspoons margarine

½ cup plus 2 tablespoons fat-free reduced-sodium chicken broth, divided

2 cups sliced mushrooms

1 cup diced red bell pepper

½ cup chopped onion

½ cup chopped celery

2 tablespoons all-purpose flour

½ cup fat-free half-and-half

2 cups cubed cooked chicken breasts

1 teaspoon minced fresh dill

½ teaspoon salt

¼ teaspoon black pepper

2 reduced-fat refrigerated crescent rolls

1. Heat margarine and 2 tablespoons chicken broth in medium saucepan until margarine is melted. Add mushrooms, bell pepper, onion and celery. Cook 7 to 10 minutes or until vegetables are tender, stirring frequently.

2. Stir in flour; cook 1 minute. Stir in remaining ½ cup chicken broth; cook and stir until liquid thickens. Reduce heat and stir in half-and-half. Add chicken, dill, salt and pepper.

3. Preheat oven to 375°F. Spoon mixture into greased 1-quart casserole. Roll out crescent rolls and place on top of chicken mixture.

continued on page 112

Chicken Pot Pie

Chicken Pot Pie, *continued*

4. Bake pot pie 20 minutes or until topping is golden and filling is bubbly.   *Makes 4 (1-cup) servings*

Note: For 2 cups cubed cooked chicken breasts, gently simmer 3 small chicken breast halves in 2 cups fat-free reduced-sodium chicken broth about 20 minutes or until meat is no longer pink in center. Cool and cut into cubes. If desired, reserve chicken broth for pot pie.

Creamy Turkey & Broccoli

   1 package (6 ounces) stuffing mix, plus ingredients
       to prepare mix*
1⅓ cups *French's*® French Fried Onions, divided
   1 package (10 ounces) frozen broccoli spears,
       thawed and drained
   1 package (about 1⅛ ounces) cheese sauce mix
1¼ cups milk
   ½ cup sour cream
   2 cups (10 ounces) cubed cooked turkey or chicken

3 cups leftover stuffing may be substituted for stuffing mix. If stuffing is dry, stir in water, 1 tablespoon at a time, until moist but not wet.

Preheat oven to 350°F. In medium saucepan, prepare stuffing mix according to package directions; stir in ⅔ cup French Fried Onions. Spread stuffing over bottom of greased 9-inch round baking dish. Arrange broccoli spears over stuffing with flowerets around edge of dish. In medium saucepan, prepare cheese sauce mix according to package directions using 1¼ cups milk. Remove from heat; stir in sour cream and turkey. Pour turkey mixture over

broccoli stalks. Bake, covered, at 350°F for 30 minutes or until heated through. Sprinkle remaining ⅔ *cup* onions over turkey; bake, uncovered, 5 minutes or until onions are golden brown.   *Makes 4 to 6 servings*

Microwave Directions: In 9-inch round microwave-safe dish, prepare stuffing mix according to package microwave directions; stir in ⅔ *cup* French Fried Onions. Arrange stuffing and broccoli spears in dish as above; set aside. In medium microwave-safe bowl, prepare cheese sauce mix according to package microwave directions using 1¼ cups milk. Add turkey and microwave, covered, on HIGH 5 to 6 minutes, stirring turkey halfway through cooking time. Stir in sour cream. Pour turkey mixture over broccoli stalks. Microwave, covered, 8 to 10 minutes or until heated through. Rotate dish halfway through cooking time. Top turkey with remaining ⅔ *cup* onions; microwave, uncovered, 1 minute. Let stand 5 minutes.

Oven Chicken & Rice

1⅓ cups water
1 can (10¾ ounces) condensed cream of
   mushroom soup
1 cup long-grain or converted rice
1 teaspoon dried dill weed, divided
¼ teaspoon black pepper
1 chicken (3 pounds), cut up and skinned
½ cup crushed multi-grain crackers
1 teaspoon paprika
2 tablespoons butter or margarine, melted
   Fresh dill sprigs for garnish

1. Preheat oven to 375°F. Combine water, soup, rice,
¾ teaspoon dill weed and pepper in 13×9-inch baking
dish. Arrange chicken pieces on top of rice mixture.
Cover tightly with foil. Bake 45 minutes.

2. Sprinkle chicken pieces with crackers, paprika and
remaining ¼ teaspoon dill. Drizzle with butter. Bake 5 to
10 minutes or until chicken is tender. Season to taste with
salt and pepper. Garnish with dill sprig, if desired.

Makes 4 to 5 servings

114

Oven Chicken & Rice

Turkey Pot Pie

1 package (16 ounces) frozen vegetables for stew,
cooked according to package directions

1 cup frozen peas, cooked according to package
directions

2 cups cooked turkey from a turkey roast, cut into
½-inch cubes (cook roast according to package
directions)*

1 (12-ounce) jar non-fat turkey gravy

1 tablespoon dried parsley

1 teaspoon dried thyme leaves

1 teaspoon dried rosemary

½ teaspoon salt

¼ teaspoon pepper

1 refrigerated pie crust at room temperature

*Leftover cooked turkey may be substituted for the pre-packaged turkey roast.

1. Drain any cooking liquid from stew vegetables and
peas. Add turkey cubes, gravy, parsley, thyme, rosemary,
salt and pepper to vegetables in oven-safe, 2-quart
cooking dish.

2. Unfold pie crust and place on top of dish, trimming
edges to approximately 1 inch and securing edges to dish.
Make several 1-inch slits on crust to allow steam to
escape.

3. Bake in preheated 400°F oven for 25 to 30 minutes or
until crust is brown and mixture is hot and bubbly.

Makes 5 servings

Favorite recipe from **National Turkey Federation**

Home-Style
Chicken Casserole

2 bags SUCCESS® Rice
   Vegetable cooking spray
2 tablespoons olive oil
1 pound skinless boneless chicken breasts, cut into
   strips
3 cloves garlic, minced
¾ cup spaghetti sauce
¾ cup prepared brown gravy
½ cup plain nonfat yogurt
¼ cup (1 ounce) grated Parmesan cheese
1 teaspoon dried oregano leaves, crushed
½ teaspoon dried rosemary leaves, crushed
1 teaspoon pepper
1 cup (4 ounces) shredded mozzarella cheese

Prepare rice according to package directions.

Preheat oven to 350°F.

Spray 1½-quart baking dish with cooking spray; set aside.
Heat oil in large skillet. Add chicken and garlic; cook and
stir until chicken is no longer pink in center. Add all
remaining ingredients except rice and mozzarella cheese;
mix lightly. Place rice in bottom of prepared baking dish;
cover with chicken mixture. Sprinkle with mozzarella
cheese. Bake until mixture is thoroughly heated and
cheese is melted, about 15 minutes.   *Makes 8 servings*

Creamy Chicken and Pasta with Spinach

6 ounces uncooked egg noodles

1 tablespoon olive oil

¼ cup chopped onion

¼ cup chopped red bell pepper

1 package (10 ounces) frozen spinach, thawed and drained

2 boneless skinless chicken breasts (¾ pound), cooked and cut into 1-inch pieces

1 can (4 ounces) sliced mushrooms, drained

2 cups (8 ounces) shredded Swiss cheese

1 container (8 ounces) sour cream

¾ cup half-and-half

2 eggs, lightly beaten

½ teaspoon salt

Red onion and fresh spinach for garnish

1. Preheat oven to 350°F. Prepare noodles according to package directions; set aside.

2. Heat oil in large skillet over medium-high heat. Add onion and bell pepper; cook and stir 2 minutes or until onion is tender. Add spinach, chicken, mushrooms and cooked noodles; stir to combine.

3. Combine cheese, sour cream, half-and-half, eggs and salt in medium bowl; blend well.

continued on page 120

Creamy Chicken and Pasta with Spinach

Creamy Chicken and Pasta with Spinach, continued

4. Add cheese mixture to chicken mixture; stir to combine. Pour into 13×9-inch baking dish coated with nonstick cooking spray. Bake, covered, 30 to 35 minutes or until heated through. Garnish with red onion and fresh spinach, if desired. *Makes 8 servings*

Chicken Divan

1 package (10 ounces) frozen broccoli spears, thawed and drained

1½ cups cooked unsalted regular rice (½ cup uncooked)

1⅓ cups *French's®* French Fried Onions, divided

1 can (10¾ ounces) condensed cream of chicken soup

½ cup sour cream

½ cup (2 ounces) shredded Cheddar cheese

1 teaspoon paprika

¼ teaspoon curry powder (optional)

1 cup (5 ounces) cubed cooked chicken

Preheat oven to 350°F. In 10-inch pie plate, arrange broccoli spears with flowerets around edge of dish. To hot rice in saucepan, add ⅔ *cup* French Fried Onions, the soup, sour cream, cheese, seasonings and chicken; stir well. Spoon chicken mixture evenly over broccoli stalks. Bake, covered, at 350°F for 30 minutes or until heated through. Top with remaining ⅔ *cup* onions; bake, uncovered, 5 minutes or until onions are golden brown.
Makes 4 servings

Nostalgia Turkey Pie

2 cups instant potato buds

2 cups water

⅓ cup milk

3 tablespoons butter or margarine

1 cup (4 ounces) shredded Cheddar cheese

1⅓ cups *French's*® French Fried Onions, divided

1 can (10¾ ounces) condensed cream of chicken soup

¼ cup milk

2 cups (10 ounces) cubed cooked turkey breast

1 package (10 ounces) frozen mixed vegetables, thawed and drained

Preheat oven to 375°F. Grease 2-quart oblong baking dish. Prepare mashed potatoes according to package directions using potato buds, water, ⅓ cup milk and butter. Stir in cheese and ⅔ *cup* French Fried Onions. Using back of spoon, spread potatoes across bottom and up side of prepared baking dish to form shell.

Combine soup and ¼ cup milk in large bowl. Stir in turkey and vegetables; pour into potato shell. Bake, uncovered, 35 minutes or until heated through. Sprinkle with remaining ⅔ *cup* onions. Bake 3 minutes or until onions are golden.   *Makes 6 servings*

Prep Time: 10 minutes
Cook Time: 38 minutes

Spaghetti Pie

4 ounces uncooked thin spaghetti

1 egg

¼ cup grated Parmesan cheese

1 teaspoon dried Italian seasoning

⅔ cup reduced-fat ricotta cheese

½ pound 93% lean ground turkey

1 teaspoon chili powder

¼ teaspoon crushed fennel seeds

¼ teaspoon black pepper

⅛ teaspoon ground coriander

1 can (14½ ounces) diced tomatoes, undrained

1½ cups sliced fresh mushrooms

1 cup chopped onion

1 can (8 ounces) tomato sauce

¼ cup tomato paste

1 clove garlic, minced

2 teaspoons dried basil leaves

1 cup (4 ounces) shredded part-skim mozzarella cheese

1. Cook spaghetti according to package directions, omitting salt. Drain and rinse well under cold water until pasta is cool; drain well.

continued on page 124

Spaghetti Pie

Spaghetti Pie, *continued*

2. Beat egg, Parmesan cheese and Italian seasoning lightly in medium bowl. Add spaghetti; blend well. Spray deep 9-inch pie plate with nonstick cooking spray. Place spaghetti mixture in pie plate. Press onto bottom and up side of pie plate. Spread ricotta cheese on spaghetti layer.

3. Preheat oven to 350°F. Combine turkey, chili powder, fennel seeds, pepper and coriander in medium bowl. Spray large nonstick skillet with nonstick cooking spray; heat over medium heat until hot. Brown turkey mixture until turkey is no longer pink, stirring to break up meat. Add remaining ingredients except mozzarella cheese. Cook and stir until mixture boils. Spoon mixture over ricotta cheese in pie plate.

4. Cover pie plate with foil. Bake 20 minutes. Remove foil. Sprinkle with mozzarella cheese; bake 5 minutes or until cheese is melted. Let stand before cutting and serving. *Makes 6 servings*

Grandma's Tip

Many casserole dishes are suitable for cooking in the oven or microwave or on the stovetop. Be sure to check with the manufacturer's label to determine if a casserole dish can be used for each type of cooking.

Quick Chopped Chicken and Artichoke Casserole

4 boneless skinless chicken breast halves

1 can (13¾ ounces) quartered, water-packed artichoke hearts, drained

1 cup mayonnaise

1 can (8 ounces) sliced water chestnuts, drained

⅓ cup minced onion

1 can (2 ounces) diced pimento

¼ teaspoon pepper

½ cup grated Parmesan cheese

⅓ cup dry seasoned bread crumbs

In medium saucepan, cover chicken with cold water. Bring to boil, reduce to low heat and simmer, covered about 7 minutes. Turn off heat, remove cover and let chicken cool in the water for 10 minutes.

While chicken is cooling, stir together artichoke hearts, mayonnaise, water chestnuts, onion, pimento and pepper in medium bowl. In small bowl, stir together Parmesan cheese and bread crumbs. Stir half the crumb mixture into artichoke mixture. Set remaining bread crumbs aside.

Preheat oven to 400°F.

Dice chicken and stir into artichoke mixture. Spoon into 1½ quart casserole and smooth top. Sprinkle with reserved crumbs. Bake about 35 minutes, until golden brown and heated through.   *Makes 4 servings*

Favorite recipe from **National Chicken Council**

125

Tuna and Broccoli Bake

- 1 package (16 ounces) frozen broccoli cuts, thawed and well drained
- 2 slices bread, cut in ½-inch cubes
- 1 (7-ounce) pouch of STARKIST® Premium Albacore or Chunk Light Tuna
- 2 cups cottage cheese
- 1 cup shredded Cheddar cheese
- 3 eggs
- ¼ teaspoon ground black pepper

Place broccoli on bottom of 2-quart baking dish. Top with bread cubes and tuna. In medium bowl, combine cottage cheese, Cheddar cheese, eggs and pepper. Spread evenly over tuna mixture. Bake in 400°F oven 30 minutes or until golden brown and puffed.   *Makes 4 servings*

Prep Time: 35 minutes

Tuna and Broccoli Bake

Chesapeake Crab Strata

4 tablespoons butter or margarine

4 cups unseasoned croutons

2 cups shredded Cheddar cheese

2 cups milk

8 eggs, beaten

½ teaspoon dry mustard

½ teaspoon seafood seasoning

Salt and black pepper to taste

1 pound crabmeat, picked over to remove any shells

1. Preheat oven to 325°F. Place butter in 11×7-inch baking dish. Heat in oven until melted, tilting to coat dish. Remove dish from oven; spread croutons over melted butter. Top with cheese; set aside.

2. Combine milk, eggs, dry mustard, seafood seasoning, salt and black pepper; mix well. Pour egg mixture over cheese in dish; sprinkle with crabmeat. Bake 50 minutes or until mixture is set. Remove from oven and let stand about 10 minutes. Garnish, if desired.

Makes 6 to 8 servings

Chesapeake Crab Strata

Salmon Linguini Supper

8 ounces linguini, cooked in unsalted water and
   drained
1 package (10 ounces) frozen peas
1 can (10¾ ounces) condensed cream of celery soup
1 cup milk
¼ cup (1 ounce) grated Parmesan cheese
⅛ teaspoon dried tarragon, crumbled (optional)
1 can (15½ ounces) salmon, drained and flaked
1 egg, slightly beaten
¼ teaspoon salt
¼ teaspoon pepper
1⅓ cups *French's*® French Fried Onions, divided

Preheat oven to 375°F. Return hot pasta to saucepan; stir
in peas, soup, milk, cheese and tarragon; spoon into
12×8-inch baking dish. In medium bowl, using fork,
combine salmon, egg, salt, pepper and ⅔ *cup* French Fried
Onions. Shape salmon mixture into 4 oval patties. Place
patties on pasta mixture. Bake, covered, at 375°F for
40 minutes or until patties are done. Top patties with
remaining ⅔ *cup* onions; bake, uncovered, 3 minutes or
until onions are golden brown.   *Makes 4 servings*

Microwave Directions: Prepare pasta mixture as above,
except increase milk to 1¼ cups; spoon into 12×8-inch
microwave-safe dish. Cook, covered, on HIGH 3 minutes;
stir. Prepare salmon patties as above using 2 eggs. Place
patties on pasta mixture. Cook, covered, 10 to 12 minutes
or until patties are done. Rotate dish halfway through
cooking time. Top patties with remaining onions; cook,
uncovered, 1 minute. Let stand 5 minutes.

Surfin' Tuna Casserole

3 eggs

¾ cup milk

2 cups STOVE TOP® Chicken Flavor Stuffing Mix
  in the Canister

1½ cups (6 ounces) KRAFT® Natural Shredded
  Colby/Monterey Jack Cheese, divided

1 cup frozen green peas, thawed

1 can (6 ounces) tuna, drained, flaked

½ cup condensed cream of mushroom soup

¼ cup chopped green onions

2 tablespoons chopped pimiento

Microwave Directions

1. BEAT eggs in large bowl; stir in milk. Stir in Stuffing
Mix Pouch, 1 cup of the cheese, peas, tuna, soup, onions
and pimiento until well mixed. Spoon into greased 9-inch
microwavable pie plate. Cover loosely with wax paper.

2. MICROWAVE on HIGH 5 minutes. Stir thoroughly to
completely mix center and outside edges; smooth top.
Cover.

3. MICROWAVE 5 minutes or until center is no longer
wet. Sprinkle with remaining ½ cup cheese; cover. Let
stand 5 minutes.   *Makes 6 servings*

Prep Time: 10 minutes
Cook Time: 15 minutes

Flounder Fillets over Zesty Lemon Rice

¼ cup butter

3 tablespoons fresh lemon juice

2 teaspoons chicken bouillon granules

½ teaspoon black pepper

1 package (10 ounces) frozen chopped broccoli, thawed

1 cup cooked rice

1 cup (4 ounces) shredded sharp Cheddar cheese

1 pound flounder fillets

½ teaspoon paprika

1. Preheat oven to 375°F. Spray 2-quart square casserole with nonstick cooking spray.

2. Melt butter in small saucepan over medium heat. Add lemon juice, bouillon and pepper; cook and stir 2 minutes or until bouillon dissolves.

3. Combine broccoli, rice, cheese and ¼ cup lemon sauce in medium bowl; spread on bottom of prepared dish. Place fillets over rice mixture. Pour remaining lemon sauce over fillets.

4. Bake, uncovered, 20 minutes or until fish flakes easily when tested with fork. Sprinkle evenly with paprika.

Makes 6 servings

Flounder Fillets over Zesty Lemon Rice

Impossibly Easy Salmon Pie

1 can (7½ ounces) salmon packed in water, drained and deboned

½ cup grated Parmesan cheese

¼ cup sliced green onions

1 jar (2 ounces) chopped pimiento, drained

½ cup low-fat (1%) cottage cheese

1 tablespoon lemon juice

1½ cups low-fat (1%) milk

¾ cup reduced-fat baking and pancake mix

2 whole eggs

2 egg whites *or* ¼ cup egg substitute

¼ teaspoon dried dill weed

¼ teaspoon salt

¼ teaspoon paprika (optional)

1. Preheat oven to 375°F. Spray 9-inch pie plate with nonstick cooking spray. Combine salmon, Parmesan cheese, onions and pimiento in prepared pie plate; set aside.

2. Combine cottage cheese and lemon juice in blender or food processor; blend until smooth. Add milk, baking mix, whole eggs, egg whites, dill and salt. Blend 15 seconds. Pour over salmon mixture. Sprinkle with paprika, if desired.

3. Bake 35 to 40 minutes or until lightly golden and knife inserted halfway between center and edge comes out clean. Cool 5 minutes before serving. Garnish as desired.

Makes 8 servings

Impossibly Easy Salmon Pie

Bacon-Tuna Parmesano

½ cup milk

2 tablespoons margarine or butter

1 package (4.8 ounces) PASTA RONI® Parmesano

1 package (10 ounces) frozen peas

1 can (6⅛ ounces) white tuna in water, drained, flaked

4 slices crisply cooked bacon, crumbled

½ cup sliced green onions

Microwave Directions

1. In round 3-quart microwaveable glass casserole, combine 1⅔ cups water, milk and margarine. Microwave, uncovered, on HIGH 4 to 5 minutes or until boiling.

2. Stir in pasta, Special Seasonings, frozen peas, tuna, bacon and onions.

3. Microwave, uncovered, on HIGH 9 to 10 minutes or until peas are tender, stirring after 3 minutes.

4. Cover; let stand 3 to 4 minutes. Sauce will thicken upon standing. Stir before serving.   *Makes 4 servings*

Tuna-Swiss Pie

2 cups cooked unsalted regular rice (⅔ cup
  uncooked)

1 tablespoon butter or margarine

¼ teaspoon garlic powder

3 eggs, divided

1⅓ cups *French's®* French Fried Onions, divided

1 cup (4 ounces) shredded Swiss cheese, divided

1 can (9¼ ounces) water-packed tuna, drained and
  flaked

1 cup milk

¼ teaspoon salt

¼ teaspoon pepper

Preheat oven to 400°F. To hot rice in saucepan, add
butter, garlic powder and 1 slightly beaten egg; mix
thoroughly. Spoon rice mixture into ungreased 9-inch pie
plate. Press rice mixture firmly across bottom and up side
of pie plate to form a crust. Layer ⅔ *cup* French Fried
Onions, ½ cup cheese and the tuna evenly over rice crust.
In small bowl, combine milk, remaining 2 eggs and the
seasonings; pour over tuna filling. Bake, uncovered, at
400°F for 30 to 35 minutes or until center is set. Top with
remaining ½ cup cheese and ⅔ *cup* onions; bake,
uncovered, 1 to 3 minutes or until onions are golden
brown.   *Makes 4 to 6 servings*

137

Shrimp Primavera Pot Pie

1 can (10¾ ounces) condensed cream of
    shrimp soup
1 package (12 ounces) frozen peeled uncooked
    medium shrimp
2 packages (16 ounces each) frozen mixed
    vegetables, such as green beans, potatoes, onions
    and red peppers, thawed and drained
1 teaspoon dried dill weed
¼ teaspoon salt
¼ teaspoon black pepper
1 can (11 ounces) refrigerated breadstick dough

1. Preheat oven to 400°F. Heat soup in medium
ovenproof skillet over medium-high heat 1 minute. Add
shrimp; cook and stir 3 minutes or until shrimp begin to
thaw. Stir in vegetables, dill, salt and pepper; mix well.
Reduce heat to medium-low; cook and stir 3 minutes.

2. Unwrap breadstick dough; separate into 8 strips. Twist
strips, cutting to fit skillet. Arrange attractively over
shrimp mixture in crisscross pattern. Press ends of dough
lightly to edges of skillet to secure. Bake 18 minutes or
until crust is golden brown and shrimp mixture is bubbly.

Makes 4 to 6 servings

Prep and Cook Time: 30 minutes

Shrimp Primavera Pot Pie

Tuna Noodle Casserole

- 1 can (10¾ ounces) condensed cream of mushroom soup
- 1 cup milk
- 3 cups hot cooked rotini pasta (2 cups uncooked)
- 1 can (12½ ounces) tuna packed in water, drained and flaked
- 1⅓ cups *French's*® French Fried Onions, divided
- 1 package (10 ounces) frozen peas and carrots
- ½ cup (2 ounces) shredded Cheddar or grated Parmesan cheese

Microwave Directions

Combine soup and milk in 2-quart microwavable shallow casserole. Stir in pasta, tuna, ⅔ *cup* French Fried Onions, vegetables and cheese. Cover; microwave on HIGH 10 minutes* or until heated through, stirring halfway through cooking time. Top with remaining ⅔ *cup* onions. Microwave 1 minute or until onions are golden.

Makes 6 servings

*Or, bake, covered, in 350°F oven 25 to 30 minutes.

Tip: Garnish with chopped pimiento and parsley sprigs, if desired.

Prep Time: 10 minutes
Cook Time: 11 minutes

Tuna Noodle Casserole

Idaho Potato & Tuna Stove-Top Casserole

2½ pounds Idaho Potatoes, scrubbed and cut into
    bite-size cubes (about 7 cups)
1 (10-ounce) package frozen peas and carrots
1 (12-ounce) can tuna packed in water, drained
1 (10¾-ounce) can condensed Cheddar cheese soup
¼ teaspoon garlic powder
¼ teaspoon black pepper

1. Bring 1½ quarts of water to a boil in medium saucepan.
Add potatoes. Return to a boil and cook 5 minutes.

2. Add frozen vegetables. Return to a boil and cook
2 minutes (or to desired tenderness). Drain.

3. Stir tuna, soup and seasonings into same saucepan.
Add hot potato mixture. Stir and serve. (Note: If
necessary, re-heat on very low heat. Add water if needed.)

Makes 6 servings

Serving Suggestion: Serve with green salad and
vinaigrette dressing.

Favorite recipe from **Idaho Potato Commission**

Idaho Potato & Tuna Stove-Top Casserole

Starkist® Swiss Potato Pie

4 cups frozen shredded hash brown potatoes, thawed

2 cups shredded Swiss cheese

1 cup milk

4 large eggs, beaten

½ to 1 cup chopped green onions, including tops

½ cup chopped green bell pepper (optional)

½ cup sour cream

1 (3-ounce) pouch of STARKIST® Premium Albacore Tuna

½ teaspoon garlic powder

In large bowl, combine all ingredients. Pour into lightly greased deep 10-inch pie plate. Bake in 350°F oven 1 hour and 20 minutes or until golden and crusty. Let stand a few minutes before slicing into serving portions.

Makes 6 servings

Prep & Cook Time: 90 minutes

Surfer's Seafood Casserole

½ pound Florida blue crab meat
½ pound cooked peeled deveined Florida shrimp
1⅓ cups chopped Florida celery
1 cup mayonnaise
½ cup chopped Florida onion
½ cup chopped Florida green bell pepper
1 teaspoon Worcestershire sauce
½ teaspoon salt
1 cup crushed potato chips
Paprika

Preheat oven to 350°F. Grease 1½-quart casserole; set aside.

Mix crab, shrimp, celery, mayonnaise, onion, bell pepper, Worcestershire and salt in large bowl. Pour crab mixture into prepared casserole. Top with crushed potato chips and paprika. Bake 30 to 40 minutes or until knife inserted into center comes out clean. *Makes 6 servings*

Favorite recipe from **Florida Department of Agriculture and Consumer Services, Bureau of Seafood and Aquaculture**

Baked Cut Ziti

1 package (16 ounces) BARILLA® Cut Ziti
3 tablespoons butter
3 tablespoons all-purpose flour
½ teaspoon *each* salt, pepper and dried oregano
1½ cups milk
4 ripe tomatoes (about 2 pounds), divided
¼ cup Italian-flavored bread crumbs
1 tablespoon olive oil
½ cup grated Parmesan cheese
¼ cup fresh basil, chopped

1. Cook ziti according to package directions; drain and set aside.

2. To prepare white sauce, melt butter in small saucepan over medium heat. Add flour, salt, pepper and oregano; cook and stir 1 minute or until bubbly. Gradually stir in milk; cook 2 to 3 minutes or until thickened, stirring constantly. Remove from heat.

3. Preheat oven to 350°F. Peel, seed and chop 3 tomatoes. Slice remaining tomato. Combine bread crumbs and olive oil in small cup.

continued on page 148

Baked Cut Ziti

Baked Cut Ziti, continued

4. Combine cooked ziti, white sauce, chopped tomatoes, cheese and basil in large bowl. Transfer to 2-quart baking dish; arrange tomato slices on top and sprinkle with bread crumbs. Bake 30 minutes. Cool slightly before serving.

Makes 6 to 8 servings

Harvest Casserole

2 cups USA lentils, rinsed and cooked
2 cups fresh or frozen broccoli, chopped
1½ cups cooked rice
1½ cups (6 ounces) shredded Cheddar cheese
1 tablespoon soy sauce
½ teaspoon salt (optional)
¼ teaspoon dried thyme
¼ teaspoon dried marjoram
¼ teaspoon dried rosemary
4 eggs
1 cup milk

Preheat oven to 350°F.

Mix lentils, broccoli, rice, cheese, soy sauce, salt, thyme, marjoram and rosemary in large bowl. Place mixture in greased 9-inch casserole dish.

Stir together eggs and milk in medium bowl. Pour egg mixture over lentil mixture. Bake 45 minutes or until lightly browned. Top with additional shredded Cheddar cheese, if desired.

Makes 8 servings

Favorite recipe from **USA Dry Pea & Lentil Council**

Baked Eggplant Parmesan

2 cups seasoned dry bread crumbs

1½ cups grated Parmesan cheese, divided

2 medium eggplants (about 2 pounds), peeled and cut into ¼-inch round slices

4 eggs, beaten with 3 tablespoons water

1 jar (1 pound 10 ounces) RAGÚ® Robusto! Pasta Sauce

1½ cups shredded mozzarella cheese (about 6 ounces)

Preheat oven to 350°F. In medium bowl, combine bread crumbs and ½ cup Parmesan cheese. Dip eggplant slices in egg mixture, then bread crumb mixture. On lightly oiled baking sheets, arrange eggplant slices in single layer; bake 25 minutes or until golden.

In 13×9-inch baking dish, evenly spread 1 cup Ragú® Robusto! Pasta Sauce. Layer ½ of the baked eggplant slices, then 1 cup sauce and ½ cup Parmesan cheese; repeat. Cover with aluminum foil and bake 45 minutes. Remove foil and sprinkle with mozzarella cheese. Bake, uncovered, an additional 10 minutes or until cheese is melted. *Makes 6 servings*

Vegetable Lasagna

Tomato Sauce (recipe page 153)

8 ounces uncooked lasagna noodles (9 noodles)

2 teaspoons olive oil

⅓ cup finely chopped carrot

2 cloves garlic, minced

2 cups coarsely chopped fresh mushrooms

3 cups coarsely chopped broccoli, including stems

1 package (10 ounces) frozen chopped spinach, thawed and drained

⅛ teaspoon ground nutmeg

1 container (15 ounces) nonfat ricotta cheese

2 tablespoons minced fresh parsley

1 tablespoon minced fresh basil

1 tablespoon minced fresh oregano

2 teaspoons cornstarch

¼ teaspoon black pepper

1½ cups (6 ounces) shredded part-skim mozzarella cheese, divided

2 tablespoons grated Parmesan cheese

1. Prepare Tomato Sauce. Set aside. Cook noodles according to package directions, omitting salt. Drain and rinse well under cold water. Place noodles on sheet of aluminum foil.

continued on page 152

150

Vegetable Lasagna

Vegetable Lasagna, *continued*

2. Heat olive oil in large nonstick skillet over medium heat. Add carrot and garlic; cook until garlic is soft. Add mushrooms; cook and stir until moisture is evaporated. Reduce heat. Add broccoli; cover and simmer 3 to 5 minutes or until broccoli is crisp-tender. Remove from heat; stir in spinach and nutmeg.

3. Preheat oven to 350°F. Combine ricotta cheese, parsley, basil, oregano, cornstarch and black pepper in small bowl. Stir in 1¼ cups mozzarella cheese.

4. Lightly spray 13×9-inch baking dish with nonstick cooking spray. Spread 2 tablespoons Tomato Sauce in bottom of dish. Arrange 3 noodles in dish. Spread with ½ cheese mixture and ½ vegetable mixture. Pour ⅓ tomato sauce over vegetable layer. Repeat layers, ending with noodles. Pour remaining ⅓ tomato sauce over noodles. Sprinkle with Parmesan cheese and remaining ¼ cup mozzarella. Cover; bake 30 minutes. Uncover; continue baking 10 to 15 minutes or until bubbly and heated through. Let stand 10 minutes.

Makes 10 servings

Grandma's Tip To freeze an uncooked casserole, line the casserole dish with heavy-duty aluminum foil leaving enough extra foil on all sides to cover the food. Add the casserole ingredients and freeze the food in the dish. Once the food is frozen solid, lift it from the dish with the extra foil. Cover the frozen food with the foil and seal airtight. Place into a freezer-proof plastic bag and securely close, pressing out as much air as possible. Label and freeze until ready to use.

Tomato Sauce

2 cans (16 ounces each) whole peeled tomatoes, undrained
2 cans (6 ounces each) no-salt added tomato paste
1 medium onion, finely chopped
¼ cup red wine
2 cloves garlic, minced
1 tablespoon dried Italian seasoning

Combine tomatoes, tomato paste, onion, red wine, garlic and Italian seasoning in medium saucepan. Cover Bring to a boil; reduce heat. Simmer 20 minutes.

Hot Three-Bean Casserole

2 tablespoons olive oil
1 cup coarsely chopped onion
1 cup chopped celery
2 cloves garlic, minced
1 can (15 ounces) chick-peas, drained and rinsed
1 can (15 ounces) kidney beans, drained and rinsed
1 cup coarsely chopped tomato
1 can (8 ounces) tomato sauce
1 cup water
1 to 2 jalapeño peppers,* minced
1 tablespoon chili powder
2 teaspoons sugar
1½ teaspoons ground cumin
1 teaspoon salt
1 teaspoon dried oregano leaves
¼ teaspoon black pepper
2½ cups (10 ounces) frozen cut green beans

Jalapeño peppers can sting and irritate the skin; wear rubber gloves when handling peppers and do not touch your eyes. Wash hands after handling jalapeño peppers.

1. Heat olive oil in large skillet over medium heat until hot. Add onion, celery and garlic. Cook and stir 5 minutes or until onion is translucent.

2. Add remaining ingredients except green beans. Bring to a boil; reduce heat to low. Simmer, uncovered, 20 minutes. Add green beans. Simmer, uncovered, 10 minutes or until green beans are just tender. Garnish with fresh oregano.   *Makes 12 (½-cup) servings*

Hot Three-Bean Casserole

Viking Vegetable Cassoulet

4 cups sliced mushrooms

2 tablespoons Lucini Premium Select Extra Virgin Olive Oil

2 large onions, thickly sliced

1 large clove garlic, minced

2 medium zucchini, cut into 1-inch pieces

1½ cups sliced yellow squash

2 cans (16 ounces each) white beans, drained

1 can (14½ ounces) plum tomatoes, cut up, with juice

⅓ cup chopped parsley

1 teaspoon dried basil leaves, crushed

½ teaspoon dried oregano leaves, crushed

½ cup bread crumbs

1 teaspoon butter, melted

2 cups (8 ounces) shredded JARLSBERG Cheese

In large, deep skillet, brown mushrooms in oil. Add onions and garlic; sauté 5 minutes. Add zucchini and squash; sauté until vegetables are crisp-tender. Blend in beans, tomatoes, parsley, basil and oregano.

Spoon into 2-quart baking dish. Combine bread crumbs and butter in small bowl. Sprinkle bread crumbs around edge. Bake at 350°F 20 minutes. Top with cheese and bake 20 minutes longer. *Makes 6 to 8 servings*

156

Spinach Spoonbread

- 1 package (10 ounces) frozen chopped spinach, thawed and squeezed dry
- 1 red bell pepper, diced
- 4 eggs, lightly beaten
- 1 cup cottage cheese
- 1 package (5½ ounces) cornbread mix
- ½ cup butter, melted
- 6 green onions, sliced
- 1¼ teaspoons seasoned salt

Slow Cooker Directions

1. Lightly grease slow cooker; preheat on HIGH.

2. Combine all ingredients in large bowl; mix well. Pour batter into preheated slow cooker. Cook, covered, with lid slightly ajar to allow excess moisture to escape, on HIGH 1¾ to 2 hours or on LOW 3 to 4 hours or until edges are golden and knife inserted into center of bread comes out clean.

3. Serve bread spooned from slow cooker or loosen edges and bottom with knife and invert onto plate. Cut into wedges to serve.   *Makes 8 servings*

Eggplant Squash Bake

½ cup chopped onion

1 clove garlic, minced

Nonstick olive oil cooking spray

1 cup part-skim ricotta cheese

1 jar (4 ounces) diced pimiento, drained

¼ cup grated Parmesan cheese

2 tablespoons fat-free (skim) milk

1½ teaspoons dried marjoram leaves

¾ teaspoon dried tarragon leaves

¼ teaspoon *each* salt, ground nutmeg and black pepper

1 cup no-sugar-added meatless spaghetti sauce, divided

½ pound eggplant, peeled and cut into thin crosswise slices

6 ounces zucchini, cut in half then lengthwise into thin slices

6 ounces yellow summer squash, cut in half then lengthwise into thin slices

2 tablespoons shredded part-skim mozzarella cheese

1. Combine onion and garlic in microwavable bowl. Spray with cooking spray. Microwave at HIGH 1 minute.

2. Add ricotta, pimiento, Parmesan, milk, marjoram, tarragon, salt, nutmeg and pepper. Spray 9- or 10-inch round microwavable baking dish with cooking spray. Spread ⅓ cup spaghetti sauce in bottom of dish.

3. Layer half of eggplant, zucchini and squash in dish; top with ricotta mixture. Layer remaining eggplant, zucchini and summer squash over ricotta mixture. Top with remaining ⅔ cup spaghetti sauce.

continued on page 160

158

Eggplant Squash Bake

Eggplant Squash Bake, continued

4. Cover with vented plastic wrap. Microwave at HIGH 17 to 19 minutes or until vegetables are tender, rotating dish every 6 minutes. Top with mozzarella cheese. Let stand 10 minutes before serving.   *Makes 4 servings*

Eggplant Pasta Bake

    4 ounces dry bow-tie pasta
    1 pound eggplant, diced
    1 clove garlic, minced
    ¼ cup olive oil
1½ cups shredded Monterey Jack cheese, divided
    1 cup sliced green onions
    ½ cup grated Parmesan cheese
    1 can (14½ ounces) DEL MONTE® Diced Tomatoes
        with Basil, Garlic & Oregano, undrained

1. Preheat oven to 350°F. Cook pasta according to package directions; drain.

2. Cook eggplant and garlic in oil in large skillet over medium-high heat until tender.

3. Toss eggplant with cooked pasta, 1 cup Jack cheese, green onions and Parmesan cheese.

4. Place into greased 9-inch square baking dish. Top with undrained tomatoes and remaining ½ cup Jack cheese. Bake 15 minutes or until heated through.

Makes 6 servings

Prep and Cook Time: 30 minutes

Harvest Vegetable Scallop

4 medium carrots, thinly sliced
1 package (10 ounces) frozen chopped broccoli,
    thawed and drained
1 ⅓ cups *French's®* French Fried Onions, divided
5 small red potatoes, sliced ⅛ inch thick
1 jar (8 ounces) pasteurized processed cheese spread
¼ cup milk
    Freshly ground black pepper
    Seasoned salt

Preheat oven to 375°F. In 12×8-inch baking dish,
combine carrots, broccoli and ⅔ *cup* French Fried Onions.
Tuck potato slices into vegetable mixture at an angle. Dot
vegetables evenly with cheese spread. Pour milk over
vegetables; sprinkle with seasonings as desired. Bake,
covered, at 375°F for 30 minutes or until vegetables are
tender. Top with remaining ⅔ *cup* onions; bake,
uncovered, 3 minutes or until onions are golden brown.

Makes 6 servings

Microwave Directions: In 12×8-inch microwavable dish,
prepare vegetables as above. Top with cheese spread, milk
and seasonings as above. Cook, covered, at HIGH 12 to
14 minutes or until vegetables are tender, rotating dish
halfway through cooking time. Top with remaining
onions; cook, uncovered, 1 minute. Let stand 5 minutes.

Tomato-Bread Casserole

½ pound loaf French bread, sliced
3 tablespoons butter or margarine, softened
1 can (14½ ounces) whole peeled tomatoes, cut up
1½ pounds fresh tomatoes, thinly sliced
1 cup lowfat cottage or ricotta cheese
¼ cup olive or vegetable oil
¾ teaspoon LAWRY'S® Seasoned Salt
½ teaspoon dried oregano, crushed
½ teaspoon LAWRY'S® Garlic Powder with Parsley
½ cup Parmesan cheese

Spread bread slices with butter; cut into large cubes.
Arrange on jelly-roll pan. Toast in 350°F oven about
7 minutes. Place ½ of cubes in greased 13×9×2-inch
baking dish. Drain canned tomatoes, reserving liquid. Top
bread cubes with ½ of fresh tomato slices, ½ reserved
tomato liquid, ½ of cottage cheese, ½ of oil, ½ of canned
tomatoes, ½ of Seasoned Salt, ½ of oregano and ½ of
Garlic Powder with Parsley. Repeat layers. Sprinkle
with Parmesan cheese. Bake, covered, in 350°F oven
40 minutes. Uncover and bake 5 minutes longer to
brown top. *Makes 8 to 10 servings*

Serving Suggestion: Sprinkle with parsley. Serve with any
grilled or baked meat, fish or poultry entrée.

Tomato-Bread Casserole

Broccoli Lasagna

- 1 tablespoon CRISCO® Oil* plus additional for oiling
- 1 cup chopped onion
- 3 cloves garlic, minced
- 1 can (14½ ounces) no salt added tomatoes, undrained and chopped
- 1 can (8 ounces) no salt added tomato sauce
- 1 can (6 ounces) no salt added tomato paste
- 1 cup thinly sliced fresh mushrooms
- ¼ cup chopped fresh parsley
- 1 tablespoon red wine vinegar
- 1 teaspoon dried oregano leaves
- 1 teaspoon dried basil leaves
- 1 bay leaf
- ½ teaspoon salt
- ¼ teaspoon crushed red pepper
- 1½ cups lowfat cottage cheese
- 1 cup (4 ounces) shredded low moisture part-skim mozzarella cheese, divided
- 6 lasagna noodles, cooked (without salt or fat) and well drained
- 3 cups chopped broccoli, cooked and well drained
- 1 tablespoon grated Parmesan cheese

*Use your favorite Crisco Oil product.

1. Heat oven to 350°F. Oil 11¾×7½×2-inch baking dish lightly.

2. Heat 1 tablespoon oil in large saucepan on medium heat. Add onion and garlic. Cook and stir until tender. Stir in tomatoes, tomato sauce, tomato paste, mushrooms, parsley, vinegar, oregano, basil, bay leaf, salt and red pepper. Bring to a boil. Reduce heat to low. Cover. Simmer 30 minutes, stirring occasionally. Remove bay leaf.

3. Combine cottage cheese and ½ cup mozzarella cheese in small bowl. Stir well.

4. Place 2 lasagna noodles in bottom of baking dish. Layer with one cup broccoli, one-third of the tomato sauce and one-third of the cottage cheese mixture. Repeat layers. Cover with foil.

5. Bake at 350°F for 25 minutes. Uncover. Sprinkle with remaining ½ cup mozzarella cheese and Parmesan cheese. Bake, uncovered, 10 minutes or until cheese melts. *Do not overbake.* Let stand 10 minutes before serving.

Makes 8 servings

Apple & Carrot Casserole

6 large carrots, sliced

4 large apples, peeled, quartered, cored and sliced

5 tablespoons all-purpose flour

1 tablespoon packed brown sugar

$\frac{1}{2}$ teaspoon ground nutmeg

$\frac{1}{2}$ teaspoon salt (optional)

1 tablespoon margarine

$\frac{1}{2}$ cup orange juice

Preheat oven to 350°F. Cook carrots in large saucepan in boiling water 5 minutes; drain. Layer carrots and apples in large casserole. Combine flour, sugar, nutmeg and salt, if desired; sprinkle over top. Dot with margarine; pour orange juice over flour mixture. Bake 30 minutes or until carrots are tender. *Makes 6 servings*

Apple & Carrot Casserole

Potatoes au Gratin

4 to 6 medium unpeeled baking potatoes (about
   2 pounds)
2 cups (8 ounces) shredded Cheddar cheese
1 cup (4 ounces) shredded Swiss cheese
2 tablespoons butter or margarine
3 tablespoons all-purpose flour
2½ cups milk
2 tablespoons Dijon mustard
¼ teaspoon salt
¼ teaspoon black pepper

1. Preheat oven to 400°F. Grease 13×9-inch baking dish.

2. Cut potatoes into thin slices. Layer potatoes in prepared dish. Top with cheeses.

3. Melt butter in medium saucepan over medium heat. Stir in flour; cook 1 minute. Stir in milk, mustard, salt and pepper; bring to a boil. Reduce heat and cook, stirring constantly, until mixture thickens. Pour milk mixture over cheese. Cover pan with foil.

4. Bake 30 minutes. Remove foil and bake 15 to 20 minutes more until potatoes are tender and top is brown. Remove from oven and let stand 10 minutes before serving. *Makes 6 to 8 servings*

Potatoes au Gratin

Broccoli-Rice Casserole

½ cup chopped onion

½ cup chopped celery

⅓ cup chopped red bell pepper

1 can (10¾ ounces) condensed broccoli and cheese soup

¼ cup sour cream

2 cups cooked rice

1 package (10 ounces) frozen chopped broccoli, thawed and drained

1 tomato, cut into ¼-inch slices

1. Preheat oven to 350°F. Coat 1½-quart baking dish with nonstick cooking spray; set aside.

2. Coat large skillet with cooking spray. Add onion, celery and pepper; cook and stir over medium heat until crisp-tender. Stir in soup and sour cream. Layer rice and broccoli in prepared baking dish. Top with soup mixture, spreading evenly.

3. Cover and bake 20 minutes. Top with tomato slices; bake, uncovered, 10 minutes.   *Makes 6 servings*

Confetti Scalloped Corn

1 cup skim milk

1 cup coarsely crushed saltine crackers (about
    22 two-inch square crackers), divided

1 egg, beaten

¼ teaspoon salt

⅛ teaspoon pepper

1 can (16½ ounces) cream-style corn

¼ cup finely chopped onion

1 jar (2 ounces) chopped pimiento, drained

1 tablespoon CRISCO® Oil*

1 tablespoon chopped fresh parsley

*Use your favorite Crisco Oil product.

1. Heat oven to 350°F.

2. Combine milk, ⅔ cup cracker crumbs, egg, salt and
black pepper in medium bowl. Stir in corn, onion and
pimiento. Pour into ungreased one-quart casserole.

3. Combine remaining ⅓ cup cracker crumbs with oil
in small bowl. Toss to coat. Sprinkle over corn mixture.

4. Bake at 350°F for one hour or until knife inserted into
center comes out clean. *Do not overbake.* Sprinkle with
parsley. Let stand 5 to 10 minutes before serving. Garnish,
if desired.   *Makes 6 servings*

Apple Stuffing

1 cup finely chopped onion

½ cup finely chopped celery

½ cup finely chopped unpeeled apple

1½ cups MOTT'S® Natural Apple Sauce

1 (8-ounce) package stuffing mix (original or cornbread)

1 cup low-fat reduced-sodium chicken broth

1½ teaspoons dried thyme leaves

1 teaspoon ground sage

½ teaspoon salt

½ teaspoon black pepper

1. Spray medium nonstick skillet with nonstick cooking spray. Heat over medium heat until hot. Add onion and celery; cook and stir about 5 minutes or until transparent. Add apple; cook and stir about 3 minutes or until golden. Transfer to large bowl. Stir in apple sauce, stuffing mix, broth, thyme, sage, salt and black pepper.

2. Loosely stuff chicken or turkey just before roasting or place stuffing in greased 8-inch square pan. Cover pan; bake in preheated 350°F oven 20 to 25 minutes or until hot. Refrigerate leftovers.   *Makes 8 servings*

Tip: Cooked stuffing can also be used to fill centers of cooked acorn squash.

Apple Stuffing

Sweet Potato Gratin

3 tablespoons olive oil, divided

2 cloves garlic, finely chopped

1½ pounds sweet potatoes (yam variety), peeled and sliced ¼ inch thick

⅔ cup chicken broth

Salt

White pepper

½ cup BLUE DIAMOND® Blanched Whole Almonds, chopped

½ cup fresh white bread crumbs

½ cup (2 ounces) shredded Swiss cheese

2 tablespoons chopped fresh parsley

Grease 8-inch square baking pan with 1 tablespoon oil. Sprinkle pan with garlic. Layer sweet potato slices in pan. Pour in broth. Season with salt and pepper to taste. Cover and bake at 375°F 30 minutes. Meanwhile, combine almonds, bread crumbs, cheese, parsley, ¼ teaspoon salt and ⅛ teaspoon pepper. Toss with remaining 2 tablespoons oil. Sprinkle over hot potatoes and bake, uncovered, 20 minutes longer or until top is golden.

Makes 4 to 6 servings

Cheesy Corn Bake

1 can (16 ounces) creamed corn
3 eggs, well beaten
¾ cup unseasoned dry bread crumbs
¾ cup (3 ounces) shredded Cheddar cheese
½ medium green bell pepper, chopped
½ cup hot milk
1 tablespoon chopped onion
1 teaspoon LAWRY'S® Seasoned Salt
¾ teaspoon LAWRY'S® Seasoned Pepper
¼ teaspoon LAWRY'S® Garlic Powder with Parsley

In large bowl, combine all ingredients. Pour into
ungreased 2-quart casserole. Bake in 350°F oven 1 hour.
Let stand 10 minutes before serving.   *Makes 6 servings*

Gratin of Two Potatoes

2 large baking potatoes (about 1¼ pounds)
2 large sweet potatoes (about 1¼ pounds)
1 tablespoon unsalted butter
1 large sweet or yellow onion, thinly sliced and
    separated into rings
2 teaspoons all-purpose flour
1 cup canned fat-free reduced-sodium chicken broth
½ teaspoon salt
¼ teaspoon white pepper *or* ⅛ teaspoon ground red
    pepper
¾ cup freshly grated Parmesan cheese

1. Cook baking potatoes in large pot of boiling water
10 minutes. Add sweet potatoes; return to a boil. Simmer
potatoes, uncovered, 25 minutes or until tender. Drain;
cool under cold running water.

2. Meanwhile, melt butter in large nonstick skillet over
medium-high heat. Add onion; cover and cook 3 minutes
or until wilted. Uncover; cook over medium-low heat
10 to 12 minutes or until tender, stirring occasionally.
Sprinkle with flour; cook 1 minute, stirring frequently.
Add chicken broth, salt and pepper; bring to a boil over
high heat. Reduce heat and simmer, uncovered, 2 minutes
or until sauce thickens, stirring occasionally.

3. Preheat oven to 375°F. Spray 13×9-inch baking dish
with nonstick cooking spray. Peel potatoes; cut crosswise
into ¼-inch slices. Layer half of baking and sweet potato

continued on page 178

Gratin of Two Potatoes

Gratin of Two Potatoes, continued

slices in prepared dish. Spoon half of onion mixture evenly over potatoes. Repeat layering with remaining potatoes and onion mixture. Cover with foil. Bake 25 minutes or until heated through.

4. Preheat broiler. Uncover potatoes; sprinkle evenly with cheese. Broil, 5 inches from heat, 3 to 4 minutes or until cheese is bubbly and light golden brown.

Makes 6 servings

Broccoli-Cheese Casserole

1 package (10 ounces) frozen chopped broccoli, thawed and drained

1 cup milk

1 cup (½ pint) sour cream

1 packet (1 ounce) HIDDEN VALLEY® The Original Ranch® Salad Dressing & Seasoning Mix

½ cup shredded Monterey Jack cheese

¼ cup seasoned bread crumbs (optional)

1 tablespoon butter or margarine, melted (optional)

Preheat oven to 350°F. Place broccoli in greased shallow baking dish. In medium bowl, whisk together milk, sour cream and salad dressing mix. Drizzle ¾ cup dressing mixture over broccoli (reserve remaining dressing for another use). Top with cheese. Cover loosely with foil. Bake until heated through, 15 to 20 minutes. If desired, combine bread crumbs and butter. Sprinkle on top of casserole during last 5 minutes of baking; do not cover with foil.

Makes 6 servings

Golden Apple Sweet Potato Bake

2 pounds (about 3 large) sweet potatoes or yams
⅓ cup apple juice or orange juice
¼ cup packed brown sugar
¼ cup (½ stick) butter or margarine
1 tablespoon lemon juice
¼ teaspoon grated lemon peel
2 Washington Golden Delicious apples

In saucepan, cover potatoes with boiling water; cook, covered, about 35 minutes or until barely tender. Combine remaining ingredients except apples in small saucepan. Bring to a boil; simmer 10 minutes. Peel and cut potatoes into ¼-inch slices. Arrange in buttered 2-quart baking dish. Core and slice apples into ¼-inch wedges; arrange over potatoes. Pour apple juice mixture over apples. Bake at 325°F about 30 minutes, basting occasionally.

Makes about 6 servings

Microwave Directions: Place potatoes in microwave-proof dish; cover with plastic wrap. Microwave at HIGH 10 minutes or until tender; turn dish once. Combine apple juice, brown sugar, butter, lemon juice and peel in 1-quart microwave-proof container; cover with plastic wrap. Microwave at HIGH 3 minutes. Slice apples and potatoes and arrange in buttered 2-quart microwave-proof dish as above. Pour apple juice mixture over apples; cover with plastic wrap. Microwave at HIGH 5 minutes or until thoroughly heated, basting and turning dish once.

Favorite recipe from **Washington Apple Commission**

Donna's Potato Casserole

1 can (10¾ ounces) condensed cream of
   chicken soup
8 ounces sour cream
¼ cup chopped onion
¼ cup plus 3 tablespoons butter, melted, divided
1 teaspoon salt
2 pounds potatoes, peeled and chopped
2 cups shredded Cheddar cheese
1½ to 2 cups stuffing mix

Slow Cooker Directions

1. Combine soup, sour cream, onion, ¼ cup butter and salt in small bowl.

2. Combine potatoes and cheese in slow cooker. Pour soup mixture into slow cooker; mix well. Sprinkle stuffing mix over potato mixture; drizzle with remaining 3 tablespoons butter. Cover; cook on LOW 8 to 10 hours or on HIGH 5 to 6 hours or until potatoes are tender.

Makes 8 to 10 servings

Tip: Store potatoes in a cool, dark, dry, well-ventilated place. Do not refrigerate them. It is important to protect potatoes from light, which can cause them to turn green and loose quality.

Donna's Potato Casserole

Sausage and Apple Stuffing

2 cups water
1 cup margarine or butter, divided
1 (14-ounce) package cornbread stuffing mix
½ pound pork sausage (not links)
1 large onion, diced
2 stalks celery, diced
3 cloves garlic, minced
3 medium apples, cored and chopped
½ cup PLANTERS® Walnuts, chopped

1. Heat water and margarine or butter in large saucepan until margarine melts. Add cornbread stuffing, tossing until well combined; set aside.

2. Cook sausage, onion, celery and garlic in large skillet for 5 minutes or until sausage is no longer pink, stirring often to break up meat. Add apples and walnuts; cook and stir for 2 minutes more.

3. Add sausage mixture to stuffing mixture, tossing until well mixed.

4. Use to stuff turkey and roast as usual or spoon into lightly greased 13×9×2-inch baking pan; cover with foil. Bake in preheated 350°F oven for 30 minutes; remove foil and bake 15 minutes more. *Makes 8 servings*

Preparation Time: 30 minutes
Cook Time: 45 minutes
Total Time: 1 hour and 15 minutes

Boston Baked Beans

2 cans (15 or 16 ounces each) navy or Great
    Northern beans, rinsed and drained

½ cup beer (not dark beer)

⅓ cup minced red or yellow onion

⅓ cup ketchup

3 tablespoons light molasses

2 teaspoons Worcestershire sauce

1 teaspoon dry mustard

½ teaspoon ground ginger

4 slices turkey bacon

1. Preheat oven to 350°F. Place beans in 11×7-inch glass baking dish. Combine beer, onion, ketchup, molasses, Worcestershire sauce, mustard and ginger in medium bowl. Pour over beans; toss to coat.

2. Cut bacon into 1-inch pieces; arrange in single layer over beans. Bake, uncovered, 40 to 45 minutes or until most of liquid is absorbed and bacon is browned.

Makes 8 servings

Green Bean Casserole

2 packages (10 ounces each) frozen green beans, thawed

1 can (10½ ounces) condensed cream of mushroom soup

1 tablespoon chopped fresh parsley

1 tablespoon chopped roasted red peppers

1 teaspoon dried sage leaves

½ teaspoon salt

½ teaspoon black pepper

¼ teaspoon ground nutmeg

½ cup toasted slivered almonds

Slow Cooker Directions
Combine all ingredients except almonds in slow cooker. Cover; cook on LOW 3 to 4 hours. Sprinkle with almonds.

Makes 4 to 6 servings

Green Bean Casserole

Baked Pasta and Cheese Supreme

8 ounces uncooked fusilli pasta

8 ounces uncooked bacon, diced

½ onion, chopped

2 cloves garlic, minced

2 teaspoons dried oregano leaves, divided

1 can (8 ounces) tomato sauce

1 teaspoon hot pepper sauce (optional)

1½ cups (6 ounces) shredded Cheddar or Colby cheese

½ cup fresh bread crumbs (from 1 slice of white bread)

1 tablespoon melted butter

1. Preheat oven to 400°F. Cook pasta according to package directions; drain. Meanwhile, cook bacon in large ovenproof skillet over medium heat until crisp; drain.

2. Add onion, garlic and 1 teaspoon oregano to skillet; cook and stir about 3 minutes or until onion is tender. Stir in tomato sauce and hot pepper sauce. Add cooked pasta and cheese to skillet; stir to coat.

3. Combine bread crumbs, remaining 1 teaspoon oregano and melted butter in small bowl; sprinkle over pasta mixture. Bake about 5 minutes or until hot and bubbly. Garnish, if desired.   *Makes 4 servings*

Baked Pasta and Cheese Supreme

Grandma's Noodle Kugel

3 eggs

¼ cup margarine, softened

1 can (20 ounces) crushed pineapple in juice, drained

1½ cups reduced-fat cottage cheese

1 cup reduced-fat sour cream

½ cup dark raisins

5½ teaspoons EQUAL® FOR RECIPES or 18 packets EQUAL® sweetener or ¾ cup EQUAL® SPOONFUL™

½ teaspoon ground cinnamon

1 package (12 ounces) cholesterol-free wide noodles, cooked

• Mix eggs and margarine in large bowl until smooth; blend in pineapple, cottage cheese, sour cream, raisins, Equal® and cinnamon. Mix in noodles.

• Spoon mixture evenly into lightly greased 13×9×2-inch baking dish. Bake kugel, uncovered, in preheated 325°F oven until heated through, 45 to 55 minutes. Cut into squares. *Makes 12 servings*

Country Corn Bake

2 cans (11 ounces each) Mexican-style whole kernel
   corn, drained*
1 can (10¾ ounces) condensed cream of potato soup
1⅓ cups *French's*® French Fried Onions, divided
½ cup milk
½ cup thinly sliced celery
½ cup (2 ounces) shredded Cheddar cheese
2 tablespoons bacon bits**

Or, substitute 1 bag (16 ounces) frozen whole kernel corn, thawed and drained.
**Or, substitute 2 slices crumbled, cooked bacon.*

Preheat oven to 375°F. Combine corn, soup, ⅔ *cup* French
Fried Onions, milk, celery, cheese and bacon bits in large
bowl. Spoon mixture into 2-quart square baking dish.
Cover; bake 30 minutes or until hot and bubbly. Stir;
sprinkle with remaining ⅔ *cup* onions. Bake, uncovered,
3 minutes or until onions are golden.

Makes 4 to 6 servings

Prep Time: 10 minutes
Cook Time: 33 minutes

Golden Apples and Yams

    2 large yams or sweet potatoes
    2 Washington Golden Delicious apples, cored and
        sliced crosswise into rings
 1/4 cup firmly packed brown sugar
    1 teaspoon cornstarch
 1/8 teaspoon ground cloves
 1/2 cup orange juice
    2 tablespoons chopped pecans or walnuts

Heat oven to 400°F. Bake yams 50 minutes or until soft
but still hold their shape. (This can also be done in
microwave.) Let yams cool enough to handle. *Reduce oven
to 350°F.*

Peel and slice yams crosswise. In shallow 1-quart baking
dish, alternate apple rings and yam slices, overlapping
edges slightly. In small saucepan, combine sugar,
cornstarch and cloves; stir in orange juice and mix well.
Heat orange juice mixture over medium heat, stirring,
until thickened; pour over apples and yams. Sprinkle with
nuts; bake 20 minutes or until apples and yams are tender.

Makes 6 servings

Favorite recipe from **Washington Apple Commission**

Golden Apples and Yams

Festive Sweet Potato Combo

2 cans (16 ounces each) sweet potatoes, drained
1⅓ cups *French's*® French Fried Onions, divided
1 large apple, sliced into thin wedges, divided
2 cans (8 ounces each) crushed pineapple, undrained
3 tablespoons packed light brown sugar
¾ teaspoon ground cinnamon

Preheat oven to 375°F. Grease 2-quart shallow baking dish. Layer sweet potatoes, ⅔ *cup* French Fried Onions and half of the apple wedges in prepared baking dish.

Stir together pineapple with liquid, sugar and cinnamon in medium bowl. Spoon pineapple mixture over sweet potato mixture. Arrange remaining apple wedges over pineapple layer.

Cover; bake 35 minutes or until heated through. Uncover; sprinkle with remaining ⅔ *cup* onions. Bake 3 minutes or until onions are golden.   *Makes 6 servings*

Prep Time: 10 minutes
Cook Time: 38 minutes

192

Festive Sweet Potato Combo

Chicken Tetrazzini

8 ounces uncooked vermicelli, broken in half

1 can (10¾ ounces) condensed cream of
mushroom soup

¼ cup half-and-half

3 tablespoons dry sherry

½ teaspoon salt

⅛ to ¼ teaspoon red pepper flakes

2 cups chopped cooked chicken breasts (about
¾ pound)

1 cup frozen peas

½ cup grated Parmesan cheese

1 cup fresh coarse bread crumbs

2 tablespoons margarine or butter, melted

Chopped fresh basil (optional)

1. Preheat oven to 375°F. Spray 8-inch square baking dish with nonstick cooking spray.

2. Cook pasta according to package directions until al dente. Drain and set aside.

3. Meanwhile, combine soup, half-and-half, sherry, salt and pepper flakes in large bowl. Stir in chicken, peas and cheese. Add pasta to chicken mixture; stir until pasta is well coated. Pour into prepared dish.

4. Combine bread crumbs and margarine in small bowl. Sprinkle evenly over casserole. Bake, uncovered, 25 to 30 minutes or until heated through and crumbs are golden brown. Sprinkle with basil, if desired.

Makes 4 servings

Chicken Tetrazzini

Turkey 'n' Stuffing Pie

1¼ cups water*

¼ cup butter or margarine*

3½ cups seasoned stuffing crumbs*

1⅓ cups *French's*® French Fried Onions, divided

1½ cups (7 ounces) cubed cooked turkey

1 can (10¾ ounces) condensed cream of celery soup

1 package (10 ounces) frozen peas, thawed and drained

¾ cup milk

3 cups leftover stuffing may be substituted for water, butter and stuffing crumbs. If stuffing is dry, stir in water, 1 tablespoon at a time, until moist but not wet.

Preheat oven to 350°F. In medium saucepan, heat water and butter; stir until butter melts. Remove from heat. Stir in seasoned stuffing crumbs and ⅔ *cup* French Fried Onions. Spoon stuffing mixture into 9-inch round or fluted baking dish. Press stuffing evenly across bottom and up sides of dish to form a shell. In medium bowl, combine turkey, soup, peas and milk; pour into stuffing shell. Bake, covered, at 350°F for 30 minutes or until heated through. Top with remaining ⅔ *cup* onions; bake, uncovered, 5 minutes or until onions are golden brown.

Makes 4 to 6 servings

Microwave Directions: In 9-inch round or fluted microwave-safe dish, place water and butter. Cook, covered, on HIGH 3 minutes or until butter melts. Stir in stuffing crumbs and ⅔ *cup* onions. Press stuffing mixture into dish as above. Reduce milk to ½ cup. In large microwave-safe bowl, combine soup, milk, turkey and peas; cook, covered, 8 minutes. Stir turkey mixture halfway through cooking time. Pour turkey mixture into stuffing shell. Cook, uncovered, 4 to 6 minutes or until heated through. Rotate dish halfway through cooking time. Top with remaining ⅔ *cup* onions; cook, uncovered, 1 minute. Let stand 5 minutes.

Company Potatoes

- 1 package (24 ounces) frozen O'Brien potatoes, thawed
- 1 teaspoon LAWRY'S® Seasoned Salt
- ½ teaspoon LAWRY'S® Seasoned Pepper
- 1 can (10½ ounces) cream of chicken soup
- 1 cup dairy sour cream
- 1 cup (4 ounces) shredded cheddar cheese
- 1 cup seasoned dry bread crumbs
- ¼ cup butter, melted

In 13×9×2-inch baking dish, combine first 6 ingredients and spread evenly. In small bowl, combine bread crumbs and butter; sprinkle over potatoes. Bake in 350°F oven 45 to 60 minutes. *Makes 8 servings*

Serving Suggestion: Serve with baked ham and peas.

Beef Stroganoff Casserole

1 pound lean ground beef

¼ teaspoon salt

⅛ teaspoon black pepper

1 teaspoon vegetable oil

1 package (8 ounces) sliced mushrooms

1 large onion, chopped

3 cloves garlic, minced

¼ cup dry white wine

1 can (10¾ ounces) condensed cream of
    mushroom soup

½ cup sour cream

1 tablespoon Dijon mustard

4 cups cooked egg noodles

1. Preheat oven to 350°F. Spray 13×9-inch baking dish with nonstick cooking spray.

2. Place beef in large skillet; season with salt and pepper. Brown beef over medium-high heat until no longer pink, stirring to separate beef. Drain fat from skillet; set aside.

3. Heat oil in same skillet over medium-high heat until hot. Add mushrooms, onion and garlic; cook and stir 2 minutes or until onion is tender. Add wine. Reduce heat to medium-low and simmer 3 minutes. Remove from heat; stir in soup, sour cream and mustard until well combined. Return beef to skillet.

4. Place noodles in prepared dish. Pour beef mixture over noodles; stir until noodles are well coated. Bake, uncovered, 30 minutes or until heated through. Sprinkle with parsley, if desired.   *Makes 6 servings*

Beef Stroganoff Casserole

Pasta with Salmon and Dill

6 ounces uncooked mafalda pasta

1 tablespoon olive oil

2 ribs celery, sliced

1 small red onion, chopped

1 can (10¾ ounces) condensed cream of celery soup

¼ cup reduced-fat mayonnaise

¼ cup dry white wine

3 tablespoons chopped fresh parsley

1 teaspoon dried dill weed

1 can (7½ ounces) pink salmon, drained

½ cup dry bread crumbs

1 tablespoon butter, melted

Fresh dill sprigs (optional)

1. Preheat oven to 350°F. Spray 1-quart square baking dish with nonstick cooking spray.

2. Cook pasta according to package directions until al dente; drain and set aside.

3. Meanwhile, heat oil in medium skillet over medium-high heat until hot. Add celery and onion; cook and stir 2 minutes or until vegetables are tender. Set aside.

4. Combine soup, mayonnaise, wine, parsley and dill weed in large bowl. Stir in pasta, vegetables and salmon until pasta is well coated. Pour salmon mixture into prepared dish.

5. Combine bread crumbs and butter in small bowl; sprinkle evenly over casserole. Bake, uncovered, 25 minutes or until hot and bubbly. Garnish with dill sprigs, if desired. *Makes 4 servings*

Pasta with Salmon and Dill

Company Crab

1 pound Florida blue crabmeat, fresh, frozen or
   pasteurized
1 can (15 ounces) artichoke hearts, drained
1 can (4 ounces) sliced mushrooms, drained
2 tablespoons butter or margarine
2½ tablespoons all-purpose flour
½ teaspoon salt
⅛ teaspoon ground red pepper
1 cup half-and-half
2 tablespoons dry sherry
2 tablespoons crushed corn flakes
1 tablespoon grated Parmesan cheese
   Paprika

Preheat oven to 450°F. Thaw crabmeat if frozen. Remove
any pieces of shell or cartilage. Cut artichoke hearts in
half; place artichokes in well-greased, shallow 1½-quart
casserole. Add crabmeat and mushrooms; cover and set
aside.

Melt butter in small saucepan over medium heat. Stir in
flour, salt and ground red pepper. Gradually stir in half-
and-half. Continue cooking until sauce thickens, stirring
constantly. Stir in sherry. Pour sauce over crabmeat.
Combine corn flakes and cheese in small bowl; sprinkle
over casserole. Sprinkle with paprika. Bake 12 to
15 minutes or until bubbly.   *Makes 6 servings*

*Favorite recipe from **Florida Department of Agriculture and Consumer
Services, Bureau of Seafood and Aquaculture***

Fettuccine with Chicken Breasts

12 ounces uncooked fettuccine or egg noodles
1 cup HIDDEN VALLEY® The Original Ranch®
  Dressing
⅓ cup Dijon mustard
8 boneless, skinless chicken breast halves,
  pounded thin
½ cup butter
⅓ cup dry white wine

Cook fettuccine according to package directions; drain.
Preheat oven to 425°F. Stir together dressing and mustard;
set aside. Pour fettuccine into oiled baking dish. Sauté
chicken in butter in a large skillet until no longer pink in
center. Transfer cooked chicken to the bed of fettuccine.
Add wine to the skillet; cook until reduced to desired
consistency. Drizzle over chicken. Pour the reserved
dressing mixture over the chicken. Bake at 425°F. about
10 minutes, or until dressing forms a golden brown crust.

Makes 8 servings

203

Spinach Quiche

1 medium leek

¼ cup butter or margarine

2 cups finely chopped cooked chicken

½ package (10 ounces) frozen chopped spinach or broccoli, cooked and drained

1 unbaked ready-to-use pie crust (10 inches in diameter)

1 tablespoon all-purpose flour

1½ cups (6 ounces) shredded Swiss cheese

1½ cups half-and-half or evaporated milk

4 eggs

2 tablespoons brandy

½ teaspoon salt

¼ teaspoon black pepper

¼ teaspoon ground nutmeg

1. Preheat oven to 375°F. Cut leek in half lengthwise; wash and trim, leaving 2 to 3 inches of green tops intact. Cut leek halves crosswise into thin slices. Place in small saucepan; add enough water to cover. Bring to a boil over high heat; reduce heat and simmer 5 minutes. Drain; reserve leek.

2. Melt butter in large skillet over medium heat. Add chicken; cook 5 minutes or until chicken is golden. Add spinach and leek to chicken mixture; cook 1 to 2 minutes longer. Remove from heat. Spoon chicken mixture into unbaked pie crust. Sprinkle flour and cheese over chicken mixture.

continued on page 206

Spinach Quiche

Spinach Quiche, *continued*

3. Combine half-and-half, eggs, brandy, salt, pepper and nutmeg in medium bowl. Pour egg mixture over cheese.

4. Bake 35 to 40 minutes or until knife inserted into center comes out clean. Let stand 5 minutes before serving. Serve hot or cold.   *Makes 6 servings*

Elegant Ranch Spinach

2 packages (10 ounces each) frozen chopped spinach

¼ pound fresh mushrooms, sliced

¼ cup butter or margarine

2 cups prepared HIDDEN VALLEY® The Original Ranch® Dressing

½ cup grated Parmesan cheese

1 can (14 ounces) quartered artichoke hearts, drained

Preheat oven to 350°F. Cook spinach according to package directions; drain thoroughly, squeezing out excess liquid. In skillet, sauté mushrooms in butter until softened, about 5 minutes. In large bowl, whisk together salad dressing and cheese; stir in spinach, mushrooms and artichoke hearts. Pour mixture into lightly buttered 2-quart casserole. Cover and bake until heated through, 20 to 30 minutes.   *Makes 6 servings*

Cheesy Chicken Tetrazzini

2 whole chicken breasts, boned, skinned and cut into
   1-inch pieces (about 1½ pounds)
2 tablespoons butter or margarine
1½ cups sliced mushrooms
1 small red pepper, cut into julienne strips
½ cup sliced green onions
¼ cup all-purpose flour
1¾ cups chicken broth
1 cup light cream or half-and-half
2 tablespoons dry sherry
½ teaspoon salt
¼ teaspoon black pepper
¼ teaspoon dried thyme leaves, crushed
1 package (8 ounces) tri-color rotelle pasta, cooked
   until just tender and drained
¼ cup freshly grated Parmesan cheese
2 tablespoons chopped fresh parsley
1 cup shredded JARLSBERG Cheese

In skillet, brown chicken in butter. Add mushrooms and
brown. Add red pepper and green onions; cook several
minutes, stirring occasionally. Stir in flour and cook
several minutes until blended. Gradually blend in chicken
broth, cream and sherry. Cook, stirring, until thickened
and smooth. Season with salt, pepper and thyme. Toss
sauce with pasta, Parmesan cheese and parsley. Spoon into
1½-quart baking dish. Bake at 350°F. for 30 minutes. Top
with cheese. Bake until cheese is melted.

Makes 6 servings

Pork Chops and Apple Stuffing Bake

6 (¾-inch-thick) boneless pork loin chops (about
   1½ pounds)

¼ teaspoon salt

⅛ teaspoon black pepper

1 tablespoon vegetable oil

1 small onion, chopped

2 ribs celery, chopped

2 Granny Smith apples, peeled and coarsely chopped

1 can (14½ ounces) reduced-sodium chicken broth

1 can (10¾ ounces) condensed cream of celery soup

¼ cup dry white wine

6 cups herb-seasoned stuffing cubes

1. Preheat oven to 375°F. Spray 13×9-inch baking dish with nonstick cooking spray. Season both sides of pork chops with salt and pepper. Heat oil in large deep skillet over medium-high heat until hot. Add chops and cook until browned on both sides, turning once. Remove chops from skillet; set aside.

2. Add onion and celery to same skillet. Cook and stir 3 minutes or until onion is tender. Add apples; cook and stir 1 minute. Add broth, soup and wine; mix well. Bring to a simmer; remove from heat. Stir in stuffing cubes until evenly moistened.

3. Spread stuffing mixture evenly in prepared dish. Place pork chops on top of stuffing; pour any accumulated juices over chops. Cover tightly with foil and bake 30 to 40 minutes or until pork chops are juicy and barely pink in center.   *Makes 6 servings*

Pork Chops and Apple Stuffing Bake

Grated Potato and Blue Cheese Casserole

    2 teaspoons butter or margarine
1½ cups finely chopped red onions
    8 ounces Neufchâtel cheese, softened
    ¼ to ⅓ cup finely crumbled domestic blue cheese
    ¾ cup heavy cream
    1 tablespoon minced fresh thyme *or* 1 teaspoon dried
        thyme leaves
    ½ teaspoon salt
    2 pounds baking potatoes (about 4 medium)
        Fresh thyme sprigs and red pearl onion wedges for
        garnish

1. Preheat oven to 350°F. Grease 11×7-inch baking dish; set aside.

2. Melt butter in large skillet over medium heat; add onions. Cook and stir about 5 minutes or until onions are softened and translucent. Remove from heat; set aside to cool in small bowl.

3. Beat Neufchâtel cheese in large bowl with electric mixer at medium speed until fluffy. Add blue cheese; beat until blended. Beat in cream, thyme and salt at low speed until mixture is fairly smooth. (There will be some small lumps.) Add cooled onions; beat until blended. Set aside.

4. Peel potatoes, then grate 1 potato into cheese mixture with large-holed section of metal grater. Fold into cheese mixture with rubber spatula (this prevents potato from turning brown). Repeat with remaining potatoes, 1 at a time.

5. Pour mixture into prepared baking dish; cover with foil. Bake 45 minutes. Uncover; bake 15 to 20 minutes more until crisp around edges.

6. Turn oven to broil. Broil casserole, 6 inches from heat, 3 to 5 minutes until top is golden brown.

7. Remove from oven; let stand 5 minutes before serving. Garnish, if desired.   *Makes 6 servings*

Acknowledgements

*The publisher would like to thank the companies and
organizations listed below for the use of their recipes
and photographs in this publication.*

Barilla America, Inc.

Birds Eye®

Bob Evans®

Colorado Potato Administrative Committee

Del Monte Corporation

Dole Food Company, Inc.

Equal® sweetener

Florida Department of Agriculture and Consumer Services, Bureau of
Seafood and Aquaculture

The Golden Grain Company®

Heinz U.S.A.

The Hidden Valley® Food Products Company

Holland House® is a registered trademark of Mott's, Inc.

Hormel Foods, LLC

Idaho Potato Commission

Kraft Foods Holdings

Lawry's® Foods, Inc.

Mott's® is a registered trademark of Mott's, Inc.

National Chicken Council / US Poultry & Egg Association

National Turkey Federation

Nestlé USA

Norseland, Inc. / Lucini Italia Co.

North Dakota Beef Commission

PLANTERS® Nuts

Reckitt Benckiser Inc.

Riviana Foods Inc.

The J.M. Smucker Company

StarKist® Seafood Company

Unilever Bestfoods North America

USA Dry Pea & Lentil Council

Veg•All®

Washington Apple Commission

Wisconsin Milk Marketing Board

212

Recipe Index

213

Recipe Index

Recipe Index

215

Recipe Index

Recipe Index

Recipe Index

Recipe Index

Recipe Index

Recipe Index

Recipe Index

Metric Chart

VOLUME MEASUREMENTS (dry)

$1/8$ teaspoon = 0.5 mL
$1/4$ teaspoon = 1 mL
$1/2$ teaspoon = 2 mL
$3/4$ teaspoon = 4 mL
1 teaspoon = 5 mL
1 tablespoon = 15 mL
2 tablespoons = 30 mL
$1/4$ cup = 60 mL
$1/3$ cup = 75 mL
$1/2$ cup = 125 mL
$2/3$ cup = 150 mL
$3/4$ cup = 175 mL
1 cup = 250 mL
2 cups = 1 pint = 500 mL
3 cups = 750 mL
4 cups = 1 quart = 1 L

VOLUME MEASUREMENTS (fluid)

1 fluid ounce (2 tablespoons) = 30 mL
4 fluid ounces ($1/2$ cup) = 125 mL
8 fluid ounces (1 cup) = 250 mL
12 fluid ounces ($1 1/2$ cups) = 375 mL
16 fluid ounces (2 cups) = 500 mL

WEIGHTS (mass)

$1/2$ ounce = 15 g
1 ounce = 30 g
3 ounces = 90 g
4 ounces = 120 g
8 ounces = 225 g
10 ounces = 285 g
12 ounces = 360 g
16 ounces = 1 pound = 450 g

DIMENSIONS

$1/16$ inch = 2 mm
$1/8$ inch = 3 mm
$1/4$ inch = 6 mm
$1/2$ inch = 1.5 cm
$3/4$ inch = 2 cm
1 inch = 2.5 cm

OVEN TEMPERATURES

250°F = 120°C
275°F = 140°C
300°F = 150°C
325°F = 160°C
350°F = 180°C
375°F = 190°C
400°F = 200°C
425°F = 220°C
450°F = 230°C

BAKING PAN SIZES

Utensil	Size in Inches/Quarts	Metric Volume	Size in Centimeters
Baking or Cake Pan (square or rectangular)	$8 \times 8 \times 2$	2 L	$20 \times 20 \times 5$
	$9 \times 9 \times 2$	2.5 L	$23 \times 23 \times 5$
	$12 \times 8 \times 2$	3 L	$30 \times 20 \times 5$
	$13 \times 9 \times 2$	3.5 L	$33 \times 23 \times 5$
Loaf Pan	$8 \times 4 \times 3$	1.5 L	$20 \times 10 \times 7$
	$9 \times 5 \times 3$	2 L	$23 \times 13 \times 7$
Round Layer Cake Pan	$8 \times 1 1/2$	1.2 L	20×4
	$9 \times 1 1/2$	1.5 L	23×4
Pie Plate	$8 \times 1 1/4$	750 mL	20×3
	$9 \times 1 1/4$	1 L	23×3
Baking Dish or Casserole	1 quart	1 L	—
	$1 1/2$ quart	1.5 L	—
	2 quart	2 L	—